Preaching With Power

Black Preachers Share Secrets for
Effective Preaching

R. Clifford Jones

Copyright © 2005 by the General Conference
Ministerial Association of Seventh-day Adventists
Printed in the United States of America
All rights reserved. Written permission must be obtained from the copyright holder to use or reproduce any part of this book, except for brief quotations in reviews or articles.

Page composition by Ken McFarland

The author assumes full responsibility for the accuracy of all facts, statistics, and quotations as cited in this book.

ISBN: 1-57847-039-0

Contents

	Introduction	v
1.	Barry Black	11
2.	Charles E. Bradford	25
3.	Charles D. Brooks	37
4.	Edward Earl Cleveland	49
5.	James Doggette	61
6.	John Nixon	77
7.	Walter L. Pearson	91
8.	Henry Monroe Wright	107
9.	Hyveth Williams	123
10.	Benjamin Reaves	135
11.	G. Ralph Thompson	147

Special thanks for
developmental funding

J.A. Thomas & Associates
Hospital and Physician Consulting

Introduction

Without question, the African American church has been a powerful centrifugal force in the history of the African American community. From the time it existed as the "Invisible Institution" during slavery, the black church has been one place people of African descent in North America were able to receive strength to deal with the often unwelcome phenomena they encountered in the New World. Yet if the church has been the centrifugal force in the African American community, worship has been the integrating thread of the African American church, and the preached word has been the most important element in African American worship.

Historic African American preaching was seldom abstract and theoretical. Instead, it dealt with the realities of life, giving hearers the hope and empowerment they needed to live in an alien and often hostile environment. African American preachers preached in the tradition of the Old Testament prophets, challenging unjust structures and policies, and calling upon political and civic leaders to not only revisit but change laws that disenfranchised blacks and others. Yet African American preachers were also priestly and pastoral in their preaching, speaking to their hearers' contemporary conditions of hopelessness. They offered a balm to soothe the wounds of their hearers, and inspired them to "keep on keeping on" in spite of the odds against them.

Notwithstanding the centrality of African American preaching in the life of the black church, attempts to define black preaching have revealed that the art form defies precise definitions. It is difficult to neatly and deftly articulate exactly what black preaching is. I usually begin the course in black preaching that I teach at the Seventh-day Adventist Theological Seminary at Andrews University with an exercise that amply illustrates this fact. The exercise begins with me showing videos of three African American preachers: Al Sharpton, a New York City minister and civil rights activist; James Forbes, senior pastor of the venerable Riverside Church in New York City; and Gardner Taylor, pastor emeritus of the Concord Baptist Church in Brooklyn, New York, and unarguably the dean of African American pastors. The styles of these three are vastly dissimilar, as are their content and audience participation and response. Asked to state which of the three is a good illustration or example of black preaching, my students almost always become deadlocked, revealing that black preaching is not some monolithic parade in which all black preachers march to the rhythmic drumbeat of the same conductor and band.

The truth is that black preaching is not something that black preachers set out to do; they just do it. If nothing else, black preaching is grounded in the African American experience. It is something that is experienced and lived, and we know it when we hear it. Black preaching does not happen in a vacuum, but in the context of black life, and it reaches its zenith in the black worship service. Indeed, black preaching is central to black worship, and there is much truth in the saying that as preaching goes, so does the black church.

Today, the pulpit prowess of the African American preacher is legendary. Yet not much has been written about the peculiar genius of the black preacher to craft and deliver sermons that enthrall and transform, and that only recently. It was not until 1970 that Henry Mitchell published his ground-breaking book, *Black Preaching*, a seminal work that included a survey of the history of black preaching and that Mitchell revised a couple of decades later. The work continues to be the standard by which all other books on the subject are measured. Mitchell followed up his pioneering work with *Celebration and Experience in Preaching*, in which he defined and analyzed the irrepressible element of celebration in black preaching. At the turn of the century Mitchell's protege and friend, Frank Thomas, reviewed and expanded on the role of celebration in preaching in *They Like to Never Quit Praising God*, concluding that celebration is the critical and integrating component of all good preaching, not just black preaching. Along the way, Olin P. Moyd published *The Sacred Art: Preaching and Theology in the African American Tradition* and Cleopas LaRue published *The Heart of Black Preaching*, two works that explored the genre and contributed much to its understanding. More recently, LaRue published *Power in the Pulpit*, in which twelve of America's most powerful black preachers discuss their methods of sermon preparation.

The paucity of published scholarly material on black preaching has contributed, perhaps unwittingly, to a heightened interest in the art form. Scholars and non-scholars, Christians and non-Christians, and young and old alike continue to be intrigued by the black pulpit tradition, asking questions that include: What accounts for the undeniable ability of black preachers to hold the attention of their hearers? Are black preachers innately gifted? Or is their competence culturally based?

In this volume, I am concerned with not just black preaching in general, but black Seventh-day Adventist preaching in particular. With our distinctive understanding of the place and role of Seventh-day Adventists in salvation history, the black Seventh-day Adventist preacher is contrained to proclaim a unique message. Yet black Seventh-day Adventist preachers cannot divest themselves of their African American heritage. They know full well that the attempt to drive a wedge between the person in the pulpit and the message he or she is proclaiming often leads to a distortion of both.

In the following pages a phalanx of black Seventh-day Adventist preachers known for their walk with God and their ability "to tell the story" are profiled. The preachers share their feelings about preaching, reveal why and how they became preachers, and tell of some of their experiences in the pulpit. More importantly, they elaborate on their methods of sermon preparation. After all, what those interested in the genre most want to know is what distinguishes good from mediocre preaching, and whether excellent preaching is the inevitable product of a particular method of sermon preparation. The preachers are refreshingly candid, eschewing all pretentions that they have all the answers. In fact, all were surprised and humbled to be included in this volume, with a few protesting that they were still learning and a long way from "having arrived." The group represents a wide spectrum of black SDA preachers, and includes denominational administrators, teachers of homiletics, and pulpit pastors. Two were not born in North America, and one is a woman.

To illustrate what they share, a sermon of each preacher is offered. Crafted and hammered out in the midst of rigorous, demanding schedules, the sermons are examples of the types of sermons these individuals preach. The sermons are not, however, to be construed as the cream of the crop, or as the best of which each preacher is capable. Additionally, since sermons are meant to be heard and not read, a fact that is particularly applicable in the black context, it is to be understood that these preachers are experienced better when they are heard than when they are read. The preaching moment is pregnant with intangible, immeasurable and non-quantifiable elements that engender receptivity and facilitates transformation, and that cannot be conveyed on the printed page. How, for example, does one convey in print distinctive stylistic elements of black preaching such as intonation and pacing? And how does one capture audience response, which plays no small role in the black preaching moment?

The collection of sermons in this volume reflects a wide spectrum of preaching forms. This is not surprising given the fact that the biblical text, and more specifically the preaching portion or pericope, often mandates the form in which the sermon is packaged and delivered. What this means is that the sermons in this volume should not be held up as the form always utilized by each preacher. Obviously, each preacher would have opted for another form had he or she tackled another passage. Standardization in preaching is the death knell of the preacher and is at variance with Scripture, which conveys the truths of God in the form of poems, events, parables, songs, and letters, etc.

Some of the preachers profiled in this volume were interviewed in person, and others by phone. The objective of each interview, though, was the same, that of learning how each preacher approaches the task of sermon preparation, and how each got to be where he or she is today as a preacher of renown. While the main focus of the book is on the "how-to" process, it does provide a window into the professional journey of each preacher, making it a blend of autobiography and homiletical methodology. The opportunity to go behind the sermon to catch a glimpse of how each preacher masters the task of sermon preparation should make this book profitable reading for seminary students seeking to learn the essentials of sermon preparation and good preaching. Pastors and preaching practitioners will find much to help them hone, sharpen and develop their preaching skills. And everybody seeking to glimpse into the mind of the African American preacher will find it interesting and inspiring reading.

Following are the dominant themes gleaned from the responses of the preachers:

1. ***The preacher is an instrument in the hand of God.*** A vessel waiting to be filled by God, the preacher is a conduit through which the Holy Spirit flows. More fundamentally, the preacher is a called person, bringing nothing but his or her availability and willingness to the task. Neither pedigree nor prowess qualifies a person to preach. "Is there any word from the Lord?" should ever be the cry of the preacher.

The humanness of the preacher demands that he or she remains connected to God, the source of both the content and the competence that the preacher needs to be effective in the pulpit. Consequently, these preachers understand the importance of sitting silently before God in meditation and contemplation to hear from God before daring to speak for God. Prayer and personal Bible study are but two of the spiritual disciplines that provide opportunity for the Holy Spirit to brood over the preacher.

2. ***The preaching event is a rendezvous among God, the preacher, and God's people.***

Preaching is a veritable encounter of the divine and human in which God speaks, the Son comes alive, and the Holy Spirit illumines so that the preacher and congregant both hear from God and are transformed. For preaching to be effective, it must be God-infused from the inception of the sermon idea to the delivery of the sermon. Self must be eradicated, and Christ must be elevated. Though a human creation, a sermon is replete with eternal implications.

A thread that runs through the testimony of each preacher in this volume is that their effectiveness should not be gauged by applause or by the number of individuals who join the church. Additionally, these preachers recognize that even when they leave the pulpit a little down because they didn't quite "hit it" that day, that the Holy Spirit is still at work and that the fruit of their efforts may yet come years later.

3. *Sermon preparation is hard work.* Spending adequate amounts of time with the passage is a necessary prerequisite to good preaching. Sermon preparation is a painstaking, time-consuming, all-encompassing activity that requires a deepening spirituality, emotional energy, and a keen sensitivity. Especially as it relates to African American preaching, the preacher must be aware of and alert to what is happening in the world around him or her. He or she must read broadly, often entering the pulpit with the Bible in one hand and the newspaper in the other. There are no short cuts to effectiveness in the pulpit.

4. *There is value in writing out the sermon.* Even those preachers who preach without any written material in the pulpit testify that there is much to be gained from writing out the sermon word for word. Preparing a full manuscript engenders discipline and helps the preacher weed out extraneous and tangential thoughts. Furthermore, it develops the writing ability of the preacher, as he or she wrestles with word choice, syntax, grammar, and the like. Good writing and good preaching are inextricably bound together.

5. *Mentorship is not to be discounted.* All the preachers in this volume assert the importance of good mentors to the preaching enterprise. None are where they are today because they sailed on their own. From the moment they considered the call to the preaching ministry, each, whether intentionally, consciously or not, paid more than passing attention to individuals whom they considered to be good at the craft. To be sure, not all pursued a structured time of reflection with their mentors. Yet each "took notes," as it were, with some following the practice even up to today.

6. *Black preaching is difficult to isolate and articulate.* As stated earlier, black preaching is not some monolithic art form. Black preachers do not all use the same template in terms of tone, timbre, etc. Yet there are characteristic themes in black preaching, two of which are that God identifies with those who suffer and are being oppressed, and that the oppressed will ultimately be delivered. Because black preaching emerges from a lived experience, it is more readily caught than taught. Furthermore, black preaching is more a function of content that it is one of form or style.

7. *The content of black SDA preaching should ever be distinctive.* All the preachers in this volume agree that they must preach the unique truths of the Seventh-day Adventist Church even as they preserve their cultural heritage. Social forces like secularism and urbanism that are seeking to derail the preaching of a distinctly Adventist message must be resisted. Additionally, black SDA preachers must fight off the urge and tendency to mimic the preaching of black preachers not of our religious persuasion.

ONE

Barry Black

Barry Black is a rear admiral and chief of Chaplains for the United States Navy who has preached before United States presidents and world leaders. Seldom, if ever, intimidated by their presence, Black knows how to expound Scripture in idioms with which his audiences can easily resonate. An electrifying speaker who is in demand as a camp meeting speaker, Black is a standout among Seventh-day Adventist preachers in general, and Seventh-day Adventist African preachers in particular. Among other things, he is known for his incredible memory; deep, resonate voice; rhythmic cadence; creativity; and Black is well loved for his celebrative style. Black holds a D. Min. and a Ph.D. and is a rare blend of scholarship and professionalism in and out of the pulpit. He is steeped in the literature in the field of preaching. The sermon in this volume, "A Book for All Seasons," was first published in the January 22, 1998, issue of the *Adventist Review*, and is reprinted here with the permission of the author.

The Interview

RCJ: When did you know you were called to preach?

BB: My mother was carrying me in her womb when she was baptized into the Seventh-day Adventist Church. As she entered the watery grave of baptism, she asked the Holy Spirit do something special for the child in her womb. The result is that I have never had a desire to do anything but preach. No other vocation rivaled preaching in my life. I am the fourth of eight children, and from as far back as I can remember, I was always preaching. In fact, I used to gather my sibling together and preach to them. My folks like to say that I tried to preach before I could even talk.

RCJ: Which preacher had the greatest impact on you back then?

BB: I admired Charles Bradford, Calvin Rock, and Leon Cox. They were the pulpit giants when I was growing up. I also admired J. C. Smith, who was an awesome preacher. Each of these men brought a different ability and dynamic to the preaching moment. They were gifted communicators who had mastered the language and who were able to engender a response from the congregation.

RCJ: What is your theology of preaching, and how do you define a sermon?

BB: I think it was Philip Brooks who stated that preaching is truth through personality. I think there is a lot of validity to that statement. I also believe that there is an element of witness to preaching. By that I mean that my story must be integrated into my preaching; my story must become a bridge to my congregation. And that is what makes preaching distinctive. The truth will never be uttered in quite the same voice. For example, my inner city upbringing on welfare will somewhat shape how I preach. Elder Bradford will bring something else, as will C. D. Brooks. Through it all the voice of God will be heard and God's people will respond in obedience. As to a sermon, it is simply the vehicle by which the truth is delivered.

RCJ: How do you prepare your sermons? What's your step-by-step method?

BB: Believe it or not, I prepare out of my devotional life. I have mastered the homiletical literature, so I know quite a bit about structures and the various approaches to developing a sermon. Each year, I try to read through the Bible. In fact, when you called I was reading and trying to put together a sermon based on my devotional reading for the day. I was reading from the book of Proverbs, and the verse that stopped me was Proverbs 16:16. "How much better to get wisdom than gold, and to get understanding is to be chosen rather then silver." I just came up with 15 reasons why it is better to get wisdom than gold, jotting them down in my margin. I have a wide-margin Bible. I've met many people who were filthy rich but still unhappy, people like the relatives of John F. Kennedy, Jr., who, though multi-millionaires, would have given up much of what they had to get him back. So, again, I preach out of the overflow of my devotional life.

RCJ: How much reading do you do for the average sermon, and which commentaries do you consult?

BB: I probably have twenty different major reference works, including Bible encyclopedias, topical Bibles, and concordances. Yet I do not rush immediately to these when I prepare my sermons. I like to stretch, to drain, myself first. I think the ability to unearth implied truth is a critical part of effective preaching, especially if you are doing a narrative sermon. Take the story of blind Bartimaeus, for example. Bartimaeus sits by the wayside, hears that Jesus is passing by, and cries out, " Jesus, have mercy on me." Town officials try to stop him, but he keeps on crying. Jesus then stops and calls out to Bartimaeus. All of this is expressed in the biblical narrative. Implied truth will state that Bartimaeus is sitting by the wayside, shedding tears, as Jesus is passing by. Isn't it wonderful that God always leaves us something to work with? Bartimaeus cannot see, but he can hear. He can hear that Jesus is coming. Bartimaeus cannot see, but he can speak. Thus, he cries out, "Jesus, Son of David, have mercy on me." Think about it, a handicapped man, a physically challenged man has the power to stop Omnipotence, to stop Jesus dead in His tracks. All of this is implied in the biblical story.

RCJ: Where do you look for sermon illustrations and anecdotes?

BB: Preachers ought to throw away books of illustrations. The best illustrations come from real-life experiences and from the Bible. Biographies and autobiographies are rich sources of illustrations, too. Anything that moves me is a potential illustration. I jot down material as I am exposed to it, filing the material away for later use. God has blessed me with a pretty good memory, so that I can recall material on cue whenever I need it.

RCJ: You mentioned earlier that you use a variety of structures to present your sermons. Please elaborate.

BB: Sometimes I'll be narrative, sometimes I use an expository structure, sometimes it'll be a propositional structure, and sometimes I use a textual structure, the proverbial three points and a poem followed by a prayer. I think it is critically important that preachers not overload their hearers with a lot of points. I know of one preacher who said that he is saying less and less about more and more as he gets older, and that the less he says, the more people remember. As I said over in Scotland, I study myself full because preaching has got to come from your overflow. Yet I never give the congregation all I have.

RCJ: How much written material do you take into the pulpit with you? What difference does being able to preach without notes make?

BB: Nowadays I take very little, if any, written material into the pulpit with me. As I mentioned earlier, God has blessed me with a good memory. When I am out jogging, I usually go over in my head what I am going to say, and I settle on devices that will help me remember what I need to. In addition to studying myself full, I also think myself clear. I go over my introduction, review my body, and settle on my conclusion. Stand up comics and court room lawyers invest time and energy committing their presentations to memory. I think preachers should do the same, and it is not that difficult to do. We preachers should ever be trying to take our preaching to the next level.

RCJ: What are some of the benefits of preaching without notes?

BB: One is that the preacher need not then be flat-footed, planted behind the pulpit. It is much more difficult to hit a moving target, and a moving preacher is able to better hold the attention of his or her hearers. Now, I'm not talking about pacing back and forth without any intentionality, but a step to the right and a couple steps to the left with purpose. I call such movement the mobility of proximity. It is difficult for an audience to ignore such movement. I noted at the recent international conference on preaching I attended in Scotland that a lot of the preachers preached from manuscripts. I do not think they were nearly as effective as they would have been had they preached without notes. The saying that "The eyes have it" is so true. If the preacher is not looking at his or her audience much will be lost in terms of feedback and contact. Having said that, let me say that there are some manuscript preachers who are still effective, but they are few.

RCJ: How important is purpose in preaching?

BB: Purpose is very important. The preacher should ask himself or herself during the preparation process, "Am I trying to inform, or am I trying to persuade? What exactly am I trying to do in this sermon?" It is virtually impossible to come up with a tenable thesis until your objectives are clear. Preachers should be able to state in a declaratory sentence what their message is all about, and the sermon is not ready to be preached until they can do so.

RCJ: Do you listen to and analyze the sermons of other preachers?

BB: I don't mind listening to others, and I did a lot of that in my early days. Most preachers do a lot of listening and borrowing starting out. The practice is somewhat akin to the training wheels of a bicycle. I do not do that as often as I once did, and there are several reasons why I stopped the practice. First, as you grow you begin to realize that a lot of what you thought was great stuff was not and is not. After a while you know where these preachers are going. They become quite predictable, and at times they are not exegetically sound. Second, it is difficult not to listen to someone and not be affected by them, especially if you listen to the same preacher all the time. If you are not careful, you'll begin to sound like the person you have been listening to. Third, there is the issue of time. I just don't have the time to listen to others, and I'd rather use what little time I have in the Word.

Being in the Word of God, listening to the Holy Spirit, will pay richer dividends than listening to mortals like me. Having said that, there are some preachers I don't mind listening to.

RCJ: Who are they?

BB: I enjoy listening to T. D. Jakes and Bishop Patterson, both of whom are on television on Sunday mornings. With Paterson it is not so much his content that draws me as his celebrative manner of delivery. I like T. D. Jakes because of what he does with implied truth and his ability to "tell the story." Jakes has some very creative ways of preaching. He preached a sermon about Hagar being sent out by Abraham with water and a loaf of bread, calling it lunch money. I think Jakes is a creative genius.

RCJ: What do you do to stay in touch with the contemporary world, and how do you make the distant past of Scripture relevant to today's congregations?

BB: I've heard it said over and over that preachers should preach with the Bible in one hand and the newspaper in the other. Preachers who ignore Easter because of its origin and the trappings that surround it err badly. We can still preach about the resurrection. Shame on the preacher who failed to say anything about 9/11. We preachers must ever be aware of what is taking place in the contemporary context, making the connection, after proper exegesis, of what the passage means for this time place and time. Yet we must be careful not to overdo it, or else the sermon will end up being nothing more than a commentary on current events.

RCJ: As a preacher, you are known for many things, including your incredible memory and voice. What have you done by way of cultivating both?

BB: One of the most valuable things a preacher can do is train his or her voice. Of course, the intent would not be to become an elocutionist, but to learn how to breathe properly and how to project one's voice appropriately. I know of preachers who lost their voices doing evangelistic preaching, all because they did not know how to speak properly. Some were able to regain their voices, but not the vocal quality they had during the first week or so. With a little investment of time and money, one can learn how to sing better and how to speak better. Something else that we preachers should shun is trying to sound a certain way, what they call "using your preaching voice." Striving to achieve that kind of resonance can be devastating. What I do to help my voice is jog. That's right, I jog. I read somewhere that you should be able to converse while you jog, so I do most of my rehearsing while I am out jogging. Thus, while I am keeping in shape, maintaining cardiovascular fitness, I am also strengthening my voice.

RCJ: What about your memory?

BB: In terms of memory, you can read about how to improve you memory. Yet the truth is that some of us are born with five talents, others with two, and a few with one. I think I was blessed with the ability to recall anything I might have heard. I can hear a sermon once and repeat it almost verbatim. It's a special gift for which I am thankful to God. But I also work at memorizing scores of poems that I can draw on while preaching. That is an area in which we can all grow.

RCJ: Why do you think you are considered a great African American Seventh-day Adventist preacher?

BB: I'm not quite sure. Perhaps it has to do with my voice. Throughout my preaching ministry I've been told that my voice does not go with my size. People do not expect that kind of volume and forcefulness coming from a relatively diminutive person like me. Beyond that, I think I have the ability to "tell the story" in creative ways that grab and keep people's attention. Additionally, because I preach out of my devotional life, my sermons, which have already warmed my heart, have a way of igniting fires in people's breasts. I only preach a sermon after I have had an experience with the Holy Spirit, the encounter giving me the freedom and power I need to preach.

RCJ: What do you do to bounce back from a bad sermon?

BB: I rarely preach a bad sermon, and I don't want to sound arrogant saying so. Now, there have been days when I didn't quite feel as though I was on top of things, but, thank God, those days have been few. I believe that a preacher should always try to get on base, so to speak, and to the extent that the preacher has, he or she has preached a good sermon. And what is a good sermon? A good sermon is a sermon that has met its objective. Bad sermons are the result of the preacher running out of fresh insights and material. For that reason I rarely repeat sermons. The preacher has a certain edge when he or she is preaching a sermon for the first time. But to answer the question, a bad sermon calls for the preacher to spend more time in the Word.

RCJ: What is your understanding of black preaching?

BB: I just completed some training with Henry Mitchell in Atlanta a couple of weeks ago. Mitchell, as you know, is the guru of black preaching. I've read much of what he has written about black preaching, and

I've concluded that what he says applies across the homiletical spectrum. The fact that an African American is preaching and that the sermon is narrative in form are not what makes a sermon a black sermon. I think African Americans bring a certain musicality and lyrical quality to what we do in the pulpit that is distinctive. We are able to "tell the story," too. These do more to identify and shape the genre that is known as black preaching.

RCJ: Seventh-day Adventists have been called to proclaim a distinct message. How may black SDA preachers be faithful to their black heritage and their Adventist tradition with its emphasis on doctrine and reform?

BB: Black SDA preachers have the challenge of making Adventist doctrines more attractive. One way we can do this is by incorporating our doctrine into the biblical story. For example, if you are preaching about the state of the dead, why not use the story of Lazarus as a springboard? Why didn't Lazarus talk about the glories of heaven after he was brought back to life? Obviously, because Lazarus had not yet gone to or reached heaven. For the four days he had been dead, Lazarus was in the grave. Preaching about the state of the dead in this context makes a lot more sense to me than the proof text method. Historically, black preachers have been able to integrate the great truths of Scripture into the normal flow of everyday life, mastering the art of "making it real."

RCJ: If you had a couple bits of advice to share with an up-and-coming preacher, what would those tidbits be?

BB: First, I'd encourage them to become lifelong learners of the preaching craft, as well as of human nature. Because the best sermons and sermon illustrations are people oriented, I'd also encourage young preachers to spend much time talking with and listening to people. Then there is the matter of the preacher's ethos, pathos, and logos, which Aristotle talked about. As you know, pathos has to do with emotions and feelings, while logos is about logic and reasoning. Ethos, on the other hand, has to do with integrity and credibility, with whether or not the preacher is perceived as a good person, as one whose life matches his or her rhetoric. Without ethos the preacher is not going to be effective. Once the preacher loses his or her moral authority, he or she is dead. Illustrations of this fact abound, as in what has happened to a few of our tele-evangelists. As such, preachers must guard their reputations and be examples to the believers. I would also stress to a young preacher the importance of studying persuasion. There is a whole field out there now that looks at why people say "yes" that preachers should become familiar with. After all, if nobody moves at the end of my message, I have not been effective, have I? Knowing the audience and its predisposition helps in this regard.

RCJ: Anything else?

BB: Appropriateness is an important matter to me. By that I mean preachers should cultivate an appreciation for venue. In other words, I am not going to preach at Camp David with the president of the United States in attendance the same way I will preach at the camp meeting of the Southeast Conference of Seventh-day Adventists

RCJ: What are some of the principles that make people respond positively to a message?

BB: They include simplicity, priority, analogy, metaphors, story telling, counter-intuitive sources and arguments. One reason Paul was so effective is that he started out as a persecutor of Christians. When he started advancing the cause of Christianity, he was the counter-intuitive source. One of the most effective principles to get people to respond positively is the active vs passive audience. The preacher should try to get an active audience. When we see preachers today telling people to touch their neighbor or to say something, it is because they know that an active audience is going to have a greater tendency to say "yes" than a passive one. Another principle is humor, though I must hasten to stress that we should not strive to be funny for the sake of being funny. Yet there is much in life that is funny, and if we get people to laugh they will be more prone to say "yes." Finally, I will counsel all preachers, young and old, to maintain their relationship with Jesus Christ through the exercise of the spiritual disciplines. Staying spiritually fit is the precursor of effectiveness in the pulpit. There is no short cut to great preaching; it does not come about by accident or happenstance.

RCJ: One last question. You are truly a celebration preacher, ending many, if not all, of your sermons in the tradition of the non-Adventist black preachers. Do you plan to end your sermons that way, or is the celebration spontaneous?

BB: First of all, celebration must be authentic. The moment people think that what you are doing is contrived or that you are striving to force a certain response out of them you will lose them. Today's parishioner is not as uneducated or as unwise as some from long ago; people today know when the preacher is authentic and when the preacher is not. Even if your celebration makes for the mild discomfort of someone, he or she will accept it if the celebration is authentic. Celebration must also be consistent with the preacher's sermon/message. As they say, good meat makes its own gravy. If the preacher has some contrived whoop at the end of the message that has absolutely nothing to do with the thematic thrust of the sermon, then the preacher is to be indicted for misconduct. Having said that, I have a couple of more things to say.

RCJ: What are they?

BB: The Bible is a book of celebration and Revelation ends with and in celebration. I firmly believe that if a person is preaching the good news, there ought to be elements of celebration in his or her preaching. Too bad if there are people in the congregation who are unable to handle the celebration. Sometimes I have had to carry my congregation, but I rarely say, "Let me hear you say 'Amen.'" I think there are better ways to bring people into the celebrative mode, like teaching them the legitimacy of expressing themselves in the worship setting. Because we've been socialized from a European rather than an African perspective, we tend toward quietness in church. Whenever I run up against this tendency in an audience, I spend some time bringing them along. Often, I'd mention the incident of the disciples being uncomfortable when that woman cried out to Jesus because her daughter was possessed. As far as the disciples were concerned, the woman was not worshiping decently and in order. I inform the congregation that before we start criticizing people because of the way they are crying out, we should first find out what these people left back home. I've also concluded that the celebration should begin long before the sermon. What's wrong in celebrating during the doxology, hymn of praise, or pastoral prayer? I think it is important for folk to see the preacher celebrating the goodness of God before the preacher mounts the pulpit.

The Sermon

"A Book for All Seasons"

In a Peanuts comic strip Charlie Brown and Lucy, as they often do, were discussing theology. Lucy said: "On the great cruise ship *Life*, some people take their deck chairs to the bow. Some people take their deck chairs to the stern. Where do you put your deck chair, Charlie Brown?" Charlie responded, "Lucy, I can't get my deck chair unfolded."

In Luke 24 we meet two followers of Jesus who were having trouble unfolding their deck chairs. They had decided to leave Jerusalem on that first Easter, perhaps to get away from rampant rumors that Jesus had risen. These disciples were passengers on "the great cruise ship *Life*." They wanted to place their deck chairs on the stern, where they could look backward at a myriad of Messianic prophecies, but disappointment kept them from opening the door of retrospection. They also desired to move their deck chairs to the bow, where they could peer ahead at the Messiah restoring

God's kingdom on earth, but this dream had been dashed. They couldn't even get their deck chairs unfolded.

This is an apt description of the human condition. We look to the past for meaning and to the future for some semblance of certainty. And it seems that neither nature nor reason nor observation nor conscience can provide us with substantive answers. We can't even get our deck chairs unfolded.

Little did Cleopas and that unnamed disciple anticipate, as they traveled to Emmaus, that help was on the way. Bewildered, saddened, fearful, they were overtaken by a Man going in the same direction.

"Why are you so gloomy?" He asked.

They stopped and looked at Him with stunned incredulity. "Obviously," they replied, "You haven't heard about the tragic events that have Jerusalem in an uproar. Our Master, Jesus, whom we thought to be Messiah, died on a cross."

They then proceeded to relate to this unexpected Traveler a tale of broken hopes and dreams. They didn't even know where to be begin. They couldn't even get their deck chairs unfolded. The two Emmaus disciples had forgotten Jesus' words, but suddenly the Stranger opened to them the Old Testament Scriptures in the light of Calvary. Beginning with Moses and proceeding through the prophets, He showed them how they had misunderstood the Messianic mission.

All too soon they reached their destination. It appeared as if the Stranger would go on. But they urged Him to remain with them. Often in our Christian pilgrimage Jesus will appear to go on. Only if we cry "Abide with me; fast falls the eventide" will our full blessing be obtained.

Jesus accepted their invitation to share a meal. And as He lifted His voice in blessing, suddenly, in the flicker of candlelight, they discerned what they had missed in the gloaming on the road: the hands were nail-pierced and the brow bore the scars of a crown of thorns. As they gasped with astonishment, He disappeared.

Leaving their food untouched, they ran the eight miles back to Jerusalem, bursting into the upper room to add their testimony that Christ had risen. The strong chains of disillusionment, discouragement, disappointment, and despair that had kept their deck chairs folded had been destroyed. They looked now to both the past and the future with optimism and confidence.

The metamorphosis experienced by these two disciples on the Emmaus road was triggered by a beatific revelation from God's Word. "Did not we feel our hearts on fire as he talked with us on the road and explained to us the Scriptures?" (Luke 24:32, paraphrase). God's Word will set out hearts on fire. His word will not return to Him void (Isa. 55:11). The proof of the efficacy of Scripture is found not so much in the satisfaction of carnal curiosity, as in the producing of burning hearts and transformed lives. Pascal correctly observed that the heart has its reasons that the mind does not understand.

Life brings to the most courageous hearts numerous stresses and strains, difficulties and demands. Ephesians 6:12 tells us that we battle against darkness, against stratospheric spiritual wickedness. The road to eternal life is difficult, and only a few are willing to walk this path of the cross (see Matt. 7:13).

Walking the path of the cross will mean encountering days when our strength is weakened, when the task is too great. We will experience seasons when the battle overwhelms and the enemy taunts our impotence. Whether these tests will end in disaster or victory may well depend on whether we too, like the Emmaus pilgrims, have permitted our hearts to be warmed by the testimony of God's sacred Word, leading us to a glorious encounter with our risen King.

The tentmaker from Tarsus experienced that encounter. He too was on a frenetic journey—not to Emmaus, but to Damascus. On that journey he encountered Jesus and was transformed into God's chosen vessel to the Gentiles. Later, in his Second Letter to Timothy, he would provide us with insights on how to meet the daunting demands of Christian living. In this inspired letter Paul told Timothy to teach the truth and commit it to faithful followers (2 Tim. 2:2). Paul wanted Timothy to avoid all idle and destructive discussions and to rightly handle the word of Truth (verses 14-16). He also urged his protege to "flee from youthful lusts" and follow "righteousness, faith, love" (verse 22, NASB). "All Scripture is inspired by God," he said, "and is profitable for teaching, for reproof, for correction, for training in righteousness; that the man of God may be adequate, equipped for every good work" (2 Tim. 3:14-17, NASB).

Paul's words in 2 Timothy 3:14-17 provide us with principles that will enable us to meet life's every demand. They remind us that God's Word can prepare us for life's every challenge. The words "adequate, equipped for every good work" in the original Greek are the combination of an adjective and the perfect passive participle of a verb. The adjective is *artios*, which carries the idea of being able to meet all demands. The verb *exartizo* means to equip or to furnish. Hence, in this last letter of a great man to his son in ministry, Paul beautifully emphasizes the all-sufficiency of Scripture.

This good news about the all-sufficiency of God's Word needs to be sounded repeatedly. Too many believe that the Bible doesn't contain all we need to survive in these complex times. We turn to the expertise of psychology, business, politics, and entertainment for answers. We seek to implement a variety of new initiatives as we apply the seven effective habits of the newest craze to men (who are from Mars) and women (who are from Venus). We seek to supplement the imaginary inadequacies of God's Word with management theory and conflict-resolution principles.

While extrabiblical resources may be useful, God's Word is indispensable. It should be our primary textbook. Yes, there are things to be learned outside of the Bible, but only God's Word will enable us to meet all of life's demands. How would we survive without God's holy Word? Neither reason nor intuition throws light on certain matters that are of utmost importance to us. Without God's Word we would know little about our personal existence after death or about the nature of the atonement. We would be unaware of the doctrine of the Trinity or other aspects of the divine nature. We would be ignorant of the way we can break sin's power and the weapons of spiritual warfare. Thank God for His precious Word.

Paul reminded Timothy that the Scriptures are able to make us "wise unto salvation through faith which is in Christ Jesus" (2 Tim. 3:15). In attempting to meet life's demands, receiving the salvation that Jesus generously offers is the most important issue we will ever face. The seminal question of living is "What will we do with Jesus?" If we fail at everything else and make it to heaven, it will be worth it all. What difference does it make if we gain the whole world, but lose heaven in the process (Matt. 16:26)? Salvation is the central thrust of Scripture. God's Word was written to give us the knowledge we need to find salvation from sin and the power to lay hold of the way that leads to our heavenly home.

The Bible points us not to faith in a book, but to faith in a Person. The Scriptures become intelligible only when we see a crimson thread running through its pages, for Jesus is the theme of the Bible. John 5:19 says the Scriptures testify of Christ. As we come to know the Christ of Scripture, our lives are transformed.

A part of our transformation occurs as we learn to see life's demands from eternity's perspective. Paul wrote these words on another occasion: "For momentary, light affliction is producing for us an eternal weight of glory far beyond all comparison, while we look not at the things which are seen, but at the things which are not seen" (2 Cor. 4:17, 18, NASB).

Many years ago my mother accepted Jesus while attending an evangelistic tent meeting. She began worshiping on Saturday, and this practice put her at odds with most of her family. She was ridiculed by my father and by her in-laws. Before she died, however, nearly every member of her family had accepted Jesus as Lord. A number of them have also died, covered by the blood of Jesus and waiting for resurrection in the earth made new. God's Word gives wisdom that leads to salvation. The Bible provides God's answers to earth's problems.

"All Scripture is God-breathed." The Greek adjective is *theopneustos*.

Second Peter 1:21 carries a similar emphasis: "For no prophecy was ever made by an act of human will, but men moved by the Holy Spirit spoke from God" (NASB). John Bengel, commenting on the inspiration of Scripture, made this observation: "It was divinely inspired not merely while it was written, God breathing through the writer, but also while it is being read, God breathing through the Scripture and the Scripture breathing Him." (*Bengel's New Testament Commentary* (Grand Rapids: Kregel Publishing, 1981), vol. 2, p. 553).

John Wesley resonated with this divine sentiment. He said: "The Bible must be the invention of good men or angels, bad men or devils, or of God. It could not be the invention of good men or angels; for they neither would nor could make a book, and tell lies all the time they were writing it, saying 'Thus saith the Lord' when it was their own invention. It could not be the invention of bad men or devils; for they would not make a book which commands all duty, forbids all sin, and condemns their souls to hell for all eternity. Therefore I draw this conclusion, that the Bible must be given by divine inspiration." *The Words of John Wesley* (Grand Rapids: Zondervan), vol.11, p. 484.

This wonderful inspired book provides celestial solutions to carnal conundrums. It provides Christians with answers to all their perplexities. And it tells how we may live above sin. It is a protection for us.

In Ephesians 6 Paul refers to the Scriptures as a sword in the Christian arsenal. It's a weapon for offense, a terror for evildoers. It divides asunder the soul and spirit and is a discerner of the thoughts and intents of human hearts (see Heb. 4:12). When I was a teenager, my mother gave my siblings and me our allowance based on the scriptures we memorized. One day a young man from my neighborhood asked me to go and help him assault someone who had hurt him. Proverbs 1:10 instantly leaped into my mind: "My son, if sinners entice you, do not consent" (NKJV). The strength of the scripture prevented me from going with my neighbor, who committed not only assault but murder. I was spared spending my life behind jail bars because God's Word provided me with a barrier against sin.

Finally, the Bible trains us in righteousness. Paul told Timothy that the Bible is profitable for "training in righteousness" (2 Tim. 3:16, NASB). William Lyon Phelps, former professor at Yale University, wrote these insightful words: "I thoroughly believe in a university education for both men and women, but I believe a knowledge of the Bible without a college course is more valuable than a college course without the Bible" Walter Knight, *Knight's Master Book of New Illustrations* (Grand Rapids: Eerdmans, 1970), p. 26.

The Bible may not hit you like a jolt of adrenaline each time you study it, but the long-term benefits of feeding on the Word cannot be denied. Its real value lies in its cumulative effects as you permit long-term exposure to work a metamorphosis in your life. As it did for the disciples on the Emmaus road and for Paul and for Timothy, God' Word will vibrate your heart with heaven's music and strengthen you to meet all of life's demands.

You can unfold your deck chairs.

TWO

Charles E. Bradford

Charles E. Bradford is a former evangelist and church administrator who in 1979 became the first African American to be elected president of the North American Division of Seventh-day Adventists. Retired and now living in Florida, Bradford was inducted into the Martin Luther King, Jr. Board of Preachers and Scholars at Morehouse College in Atlanta, Georgia, in 1994. Bradford, or "Brad," as he is affectionately called, is a prolific author whose books include *Preaching to the Times*, a preaching text which though published over twenty years ago is still relevant today, and *Sabbath Roots: The African Connection*, in which Bradford explores the history of the Sabbath on the African continent. An entire generation of preachers grew up admiring Bradford, whose wit, wisdom, and wealth of theology still make him a regular on the camp meeting circuit. In 2002, Oakwood College, Bradford's alma mater, launched a campaign to establish the Bradford-Cleveland Institute on its campus. Named in honor of Bradford and E. E. Cleveland, unarguably Adventism's most renowned evangelist, the Institute will be a continuing education center intended to facilitate life-long learning in the areas of pastoral ministry, biblical studies, and evangelism.

The Interview

RCJ: Did you always want to be a preacher?
CEB: I was raised in the home of an Adventist preacher, but it was not until my sophomore year in college that I made the decision to become one myself. You see, I wanted to be a physician and was encouraged in that direction by a benefactor friend of the family from Philadelphia, Pennsylvania. The truth is, though, that in those days there weren't as many opportunities or possibilities for young black men. Preaching was it, and being surrounded by so many preachers and potential preachers at

Oakwood College certainly influenced my decision to become a preacher.

RCJ: Which preachers had an influence on you in your early days?

CEB: My dad was a Seventh-day Adventist minister, and, of course, he made the first impression on me. I heard him a lot and appreciated his preaching. Other men who had a tremendous influence on me included George Peters, W. W. Fordham, and W. S. Lee, Sr. You will notice, I'm sure, that they were all Adventist. Unfortunately, I am unable to recall the preacher who had the greatest influence on me back then, though I do remember that he was ministering in Boston at the time and that the president of the New Jersey Conference once referred to him as one of Adventism's finest preachers. These men impressed me both because of their content and their style, and, quite understandably, some impressed me more than others.

RCJ: In your book, *Preaching to the Times*, you indicate that preachers need to develop a tenable theology of preaching. What is your theology of preaching?

CEB: My theology of preaching tells me the sermon comes from God. God is the source of all preaching, and without God there is no need to preach. Preaching is not the all-in-all of ministry, but one activity among many. I fully resonate with the contemporary feeling that the community of faith is really a preaching community itself. The preacher is one among many, the leader perhaps of the worship service. But the preacher is not the owner of the congregation or the service. My assessment of the sermon is that it is an attempt to reach out to the people in the context of Ephesians 4, especially verses 11 and 13.

RCJ: How do you tackle the task of sermon preparation?

CEB: I am indebted to the New York Theological Seminary and have tried to implement what they have taught there for years. I begin my brooding over the Scriptural passage, observing words, events, thoughts, and nuances. Now, observation is not the same thing as mind wondering. My observation and study lead me to the development of the theme. I believe that one can develop a theme from any Bible passage. Once I have developed a theme I jot down an outline, which I will let sit for a few days. I fill in the details, sort of like putting flesh on the bones, after that. Now, sometimes the first steps in my sermon preparation process take place concurrently, not sequentially.

RCJ: How long does it take you to prepare a sermon on average?

CEB: When I was a young preacher in Louisiana, an old gentleman told me that to get a good crop of strawberries, you have to work at it for a year. Preparing the soil, applying fertilizer, and tending to the crop call for patience and hard work, he told me. It seems to me that preparing a good sermon takes about as long. You just have to keep working at a sermon, cultivating it, pruning it, making sure there is movement. Good sermons do not just happen, and they certainly can't be put together overnight or in a few hours. It takes painstaking effort.

RCJ: Is your reading program regular and consistent? Do you have a program of general and specific reading?

CEB: I have to confess that my reading program is not what it ought to be. In my library at home are some of the well-known Commentaries—the *Anchor Bible Commentary,* and the *Cambridge Commentary.* Of course, our own *Seventh-day Adventist Bible Commentary* is there, too. I try to consult these in preparing my sermons, as well as other sources. I do read, I think, broadly, especially when I am traveling and need to while away the time. But I must admit that my reading is not what I would like it to be. I have to do better in that regard.

RCJ: You have been preaching for over fifty years. What are some of the practices and skills you still utilize today?

CEB: In the past, I would sometimes read my sermons out loud, practicing my preaching that way. Now, the only time I may do this is when I am in the shower. As far as picking up a manuscript and re-reading it before entering the pulpit, I don't do much of that today. What I still do is read my lines before going to bed. I heard somewhere that that is something great actors do because it drives the material into the subconscious.

RCJ: How has preaching changed in the fifty years you've been preaching?

CEB: Seventh-day Adventist preaching has changed dramatically. As a youngster coming up, Adventist preachers were more reserved. They avoided anything that triggered the emotions. Today, preachers encourage clapping, shouting, and other things that convey emotional states. I remember my father saying to me, "Son, you're sounding like a Baptist minister." I tried to convince my dad that I was being careful not to, but the truth is that I don't know how careful I really was. Has the audience changed? Yes, if in no other way than in size. When I began preaching in Louisiana, if you had an audience of 100 you had a pretty good size church. We had a church in Monroe, Louisiana, with a membership of three. One was confined to a wheelchair and the other two lived out in the country. I was looked on with envy because I had a church of 150. In New Rochelle, New York, I had about 85 members. The only truly big churches back then were Bethel in Brooklyn, and Ephesus in Manhattan. There wasn't even the City Tabernacle Church in Manhattan then. So one thing that has changed is the size of our congregation and that makes for a corresponding change in preaching.

RCJ: How so?

CEB: Let me illustrate by telling of something that happened some time ago. I met a woman in Tampa, Florida, who informed me that she used to be an Adventist. When I asked about her current church affiliation she told me that she had joined one of those large, charismatic churches that started with less than 100 but in ten to fifteen years had ballooned to over 4000. The kind of preaching that appeals to folk like this woman is the gospel of wealth and success, a kind of pop psychology. Some Adventist preachers today seem to be giving in to the temptation to preach a goody, goody gospel that contributes to a feeling of ease. Yet Ellen While says to us, "Brethren, sharpen up your message. Sharpen up your message." And she reminds us that it would be better to give a Bible study than to engage in sickly preaching. A sickly offering is preaching that does not contain Bible truth though done with eloquence.

RCJ: What about the makeup of the congregation?

CEB: I believe that we have more professionals in our congregations today, partly due to the fact that people are more education conscious. It is a different world in which we live and preach today. Ours is a world in which it seems everything has been speeded up. Today, to be relevant preachers must be informed and cutting edge. They must keep their fingers on the pulse of society, being knowledgeable and conversant with contemporary events and issues.

RCJ: How do you keep your preaching contemporary and alive?

CEB: It's all about service. Preachers are there to serve the people. Consequently, they should go to lengths to understand where people are and what they are going through. All of us think a little more creatively when we have some idea of what is needed and where we are going. Preaching is not a classroom lecture. We must make the connection with people.

RCJ: How do you decide what to preach when you have not been assigned a topic or theme?

CEB: Old Elder Peters used to say, "Now boys, don't read the newspaper on Sabbath, but be sure to look at the headlines." In those days every Adventist sermon seemed to be on the Second Coming. I won't criticize those preachers too much because they were under the conviction that the end was very imminent. Yet, to take the old man's counsel seriously, we preachers have before us a gold mine of possibilities for sermons in the news of the day. The other day I preached a sermon entitled "Invest in Enron?" It was based on Romans 5 and my theme was that Christ invested in us, though we were all bankrupt. I argued that Justification is nothing but a great deposit of Christ's righteousness that Christ Himself has put on our account, and that Sanctification is nothing else but Christ giving each of us an ATM card that we can use to withdraw a daily supply of His righteousness.

RCJ: In *Preaching to the Times,* that wonderful book that you wrote back in 1975, you stated that more important than the preparation of the sermon is the preparation of the preacher. As I recall, you stated that it takes more than three or four hours a week for the preacher to prepare himself or herself. Please share how you prepare yourself to preach?

CEB: Unfortunately, we Seventh-day Adventists have not been deep into the mystical disciplines. I wasn't always a big fan of Oswald Chambers, who wrote that great book, *My Utmost for His Highest.* I have that book on computer, and I read a little bit of it each time I sit down at my computer. I especially like reading it in the morning. I am retired now, and that means that I have a lot of time at my disposal. So finding time to meditate and read is not a problem for me, as it is for the busy pastor in the pew. Besides reading and meditating, I spend an inordinate amount of time in prayer. I recognize that spending time alone with God is vitally important to good, effective preaching, and that the preacher who neglects to engage in the spiritual disciplines does so at his or her own peril.

RCJ: Back to *Preaching to the Times,* you state in the book that once in the pulpit the preacher must forget all the rules of rhetoric and technique. What do you mean?

CEB: Elder Singleton, one of Adventism's great titans, icons, and role models, was a preacher who could not preach his way out of a paper bag. Singleton wanted to be a great golfer, though he was not very athletic. He paid attention to what the other golfers did, and had the practice of removing from his pocket a piece of paper, on which was inscribed his golfing notes, and reading his notes before striking the ball. Needless to say, we used to laugh at old man Singleton. From those experiences I learned that the preacher's technique should be so much a part of him or her that he or she does not need to whip out notes on preaching as he or she stands in the pulpit. That is what I meant when I stated that once in the pulpit the preacher must forget about rhetoric and technique.

RCJ: Are you basically a topical, textual, or expository preacher?

CEB: I often wonder who it was that decided to categorize sermons as textual, topical, and expository. I am not sure what I am generally or principally. What I do know is that I want to be effective in the pulpit and that I try to do whatever makes for optimum effectiveness. I had some of my most memorable ministerial experiences in St. Louis, Missouri. One Sabbath afternoon I asked a group of young men learning Homiletics to identify the type of sermon I had just preached. They were unable to say if the sermon was topical, textual, or expository, to which I responded, "Listen, guys, you've got to learn the trade before you learn the tricks of the trade." I do not want to be oblivious to or discount the reality that there are different forms of sermons based on the biblical text, but I do believe that we should not be stuck to these modalities. What I strive for in the pulpit is effectiveness, and as the pitching coach once told a rookie pitcher, "If you have a good fastball, I can teach you the curve ball."

RCJ: Along those lines, are you a manuscript preacher, and what difference do you think preaching without notes makes?

CEB: Allow me to return to the world of baseball. Let's say that a hitter is doing well at the plate. The guy is hitting home runs, triples, doubles, everything, yet the guy is holding the bat the wrong way. A purist comes along and says to the hitter, "Hey, you're holding the bat the wrong way. This is the correct way to hold a baseball bat." Does that make sense? The guy is already hitting home runs, which is the object of any hitter. What good is it to tamper with the style, if not career, of the hitter? Why flirt with the possibility of destroying a good thing? There are manuscript preachers who can preach up a storm. One of them was W. W. Fordham, who, though a great evangelist of the first order, read his sermons. Fordham used to point at his manuscript with his finger, while holding down his manuscript with his other hand. Yet he never missed a phrase or sentence and was as eloquent as you could wish a speaker to be. Even today, I could never do that.

RCJ: What role does personality play in preaching?

CEB: I don't think it is possible to circumvent personality, can you? We are not robots or automatons, but people, and it is a real person who enters the pulpit, a flesh-and-blood person. The only times I fell flat on my face in the pulpit were those in which I tried to be somebody else. What preachers need to understand is that, in spite of our varied styles, we can all still be effective. Take George Vandeman for example. You cannot tell me that he was not effective. Neither can anyone say that R. T. Hudson, the former New York City powerhouse, was not effective. These two preachers, men of different personalities, were both effective. Vandeman was low-key, while Hudson was so loud that people often went home with a ring in their ears.

RCJ: Much ado has been made about black preaching. What is your understanding of black preaching?

CEB: Well, we named it black preaching, didn't we? I think black preaching is that preaching that is acutely aware of issues with which the African American community resonates. In other words, issues are the most characteristic features of black preaching. The gospel, however, is bigger than a black or white issue. You know that song whose lyrics include the words, "Somebody bigger than you or I?" Well, the gospel is bigger than black and white. I cannot preach as though black issues were the total gospel. Our message is God; it is "Fear God, and give glory to Him for the hour of His judgement has come." So God is first, and God cannot be dichotomized or compartmentalized. God says to us preachers, "Preach My gospel, whether you are Japanese or from the east or west. I will help to make you effective in any climate or nation, and among any people or language." So if there is such a thing as black theology and black preaching, and I believe that there are, the gospel transcends them.

RCJ: How would you like to be remembered as a preacher?

CEB: I am reminded of a preacher of yesteryear who ministered in Cincinnati, Ohio. He was from the east and was not well liked in Ohio because in those days Ohio was frontier territory. Utterly discouraged, the preacher almost gave up on preaching, finally deciding to hold on. "I will not worry about style and all that stuff," he stated, "I am just going to be helpful to people." That decision changed his preaching and the course of his ministerial career. That is how I want to be remembered as a preacher, as someone who was helpful. There is much talk among Adventists today about the health care ministry. Well, we preachers are in the health care ministry of the soul. We are here to help people, who want to know that the preacher is with them in their struggles. They want to know that the preacher understands and cares. Preaching is nothing but one beggar giving another beggar sympathy and empathy. The great preacher Henry Fosdick used to say that people do not what to know so much what happened to the Jebusites, but the meaning of it all and how it applies to their lives. It is a tragedy for a preacher to have perfect pronunciation, enunciation, emphasis, rhetoric, yet get to the end of his or her sermon and discover that the people are not there.

RCJ: What advice do you have for young preachers?

CEB: When I was a student at Oakwood, our college physician was a man from Pittsburg, Pennsylvania. He was a nice man who allowed some of us guys to use his car, an Oldsmobile at the time. As I was walking across campus one day, I ran into the good doctor. As our paths crossed, he started laughing, and picking up a piece of paper from the ground, he said, "Son, you're a pretty good preacher, but there are three things you must be on the lookout for if you are to succeed in the preaching ministry." The doctor then drew what looked like a three-legged animal on the piece of paper, with a poor preacher hanging from the creature. He identified the three legs of the creature as money, women, and appetite. Beyond that, I would encourage young preachers to get and stay in the Word. I would also encourage them to know themselves, and to resist the temptation to try to be what they are not in the pulpit. Authenticity will go a long way in making for an effective sermon. On the other hand, if a congregation suspects that they are witnessing a charade, the preacher is doomed.

RCJ: Is there anything else?

CEB: As preachers, we must love people, visiting and caring for them. The preacher that is in touch with the needs of his or her people will ever be loved by them. He or she may not be a power ball in the pulpit in terms of homiletical skills, but he or she will be tall in stature. Preachers should strive to always make the truth they proclaim relevant, living what they preach. Consistently in life and leadership is critical. We must take our work seriously, working when it is time to work, and playing when it is time to play. Let me hasten to add that even though we must take our work seriously, we should not take ourselves seriously. Finally, and this may sound strange, but we must be sure not to make preaching detract from our mission, which is equipping the saints for ministry and preparing them for the soon return of Jesus Christ. In this regard, the gifts of the preacher may not be many, but he or she must never forget that the Holy Spirit is the primary medium of empowerment.

The Sermon

""Guess Who's Coming to Dinner?"

"**Jesus went through one town and village after another, teaching as he made his way to Jerusalem. Someone asked him, "Lord, will only a few be saved?" He said to them, "Strive to enter through the narrow door; for many, I tell you, will try to enter and will not be able**" (Luke 13:22-24 NRSV).

Jesus is on His way to Jerusalem, preaching, teaching and healing as He goes. His earthly ministry is rapidly coming to a close. Totally absorbed in His mission, His words take on new meaning and urgency. He challenges the powers of darkness, throwing down the gauntlet as it were. "I will drive out demons and heal people today and tomorrow, and on the third day I will reach my goal . . . I must keep going!" His words are so direct and personal and pointed that one of His hearers cries out, "Lord, are only a few people going to be saved?" It is a diversionary tactic, to be sure. But it doesn't work. Jesus will not be detoured. He answers at once, "Strive to enter in at the strait gate, for many, I say unto you, will seek to enter in, and shall not be able." The issue at hand is preparation for entrance into the kingdom. Speculation as to who will enter and how many are going to make up the number is irrelevant. "People get ready!" is the message.

The preacher's out of touch

The religious leaders of the day had become irrelevant, out of touch with the realities around them. They spoke of a paradise to come, a place of beautiful gardens, crystal ponds and fountains, and numerous banquet halls where never-ending feasts took place. Of course, this was only for a chosen few. The masses had been taught so, and they had come to believe it. "We are Abraham's children; it is bloodline that counts." One of the popular sayings of the day was, "Earth is for the many, but heaven is for the few." Only the elect could expect to enjoy the paradise of God. All others were excluded from the blissful state.

But Jesus came preaching a radically different message. He swept away the treasured legacy and called for repentance. What Jesus really said may be summarized in the following: "In my kingdom what counts is a spirit of poverty." Jesus said, "Blessed are the poor in spirit; for theirs is the kingdom of heaven" (Matt. 5:3 KJV). The followers of Jesus must first declare spiritual bankruptcy; they must renounce all privilege. In the kingdom of Jesus there is no such thing as favored nation status. It is fatal to assume that we are on the inside track on our way there.

Indeed, the door to the kingdom of Jesus is narrow. The gate is straight. Few are able to find it, and those who do know what is required to enter. They know that it calls for discipline and self-denial. They know that they must be serious about it, that nothing can be taken for granted, that soberness and vigilance will always be in order. They know that they cannot nonchalantly saunter along, taking the grace of God for granted. Like the eye of the needle, the straight gate demands that all excess baggage be laid aside.

Radical Message—Radical Change

Some things must be put off. Others must literally be stripped off. "Put off your old self, which is being corrupted by its deceitful desires; to be made new in the attitude of your minds; and to put on the new self, created to be life God in true righteousness and holiness" (Eph. 4:22, 24 NIV). "If your right eye causes you to sin, tear it out and throw it away" (Matt. 5:29 NRSV).

Far too many 21st century Christians haven't the foggiest notion about discipleship and cross bearing. Today we have a pop culture and a pop religion. According to Elizabeth Achtemeir, if the preacher were to begin his sermon in some sophisticated congregations by saying, "Take up your cross." several will respond with, "Wait a minute. I'll get the SUV and pick it up." Today's religious leaders preach a kind of civic religion, and some have gone so far as to say that we are a Christian nation. The result is a warm, cozy, blanket religion. All the blessings we enjoy are thought to be our heritage, our national right. The people of the land assume that they have it made, that our good deeds and good religious feelings will be rewarded with a place in the kingdom. But Jesus jars us back to reality. "For many I say unto you, will seek to enter in, and shall not be able." The way is narrow.

Rude Awakening

Please keep in mind that Jesus was preaching to religious people. These people were often to be found in the synagogues and even in the temple. They were not barbarians. Yet Jesus puts His message on a sign board and holds it up for them to read so that they cannot miss it. "Once the owner of the house gets up and closes the door, you will stand outside knocking and pleading, 'Sir, open the door for us.' But he will answer, 'I don't know you or where you come from'" (Luke 13:25 NIV). How can they be outside when they are the real insiders?

I once heard the story of a young female attorney who was the pride of the crown colony where she lived. Not wearing the robe and wig that was required in those days, she once rushed into court late to defend a client. After a long pause, the old judge said to her, "Where is the counsel for the defense?" "I am here," the young barrister replied, standing before him. Peering over his horn-rimmed glasses, the judge intoned, "I do not recognize her."

Jesus is preaching to an entire nation. He is doing His best to save His people from national ruin. He is on His way to the showdown in Jerusalem. Time is running out. Soon Jesus will preach in the very shadows of the temple, "O Jerusalem, Jerusalem, you who kill the prophets and stone those sent to you, how often I have longed to gather your children together, as a hen gathers her chicks under her wings, but you were not willing" (Luke 13:34 NIV). There is urgency! A time frame, a window of opportunity, exists. But it will not be there for long. Soon the door will be shut. As in the parable of the ten virgins, some will be left outside the closed door. Some will hear the pronouncement, "I don't know you."

What is the thing that is most essential in this preparation for which Jesus is calling? His words are plain enough. "Now this is eternal life; that they may know you, the only true God, and Jesus Christ, whom you have sent" (John 17:3 NIV). No wonder the apostle Paul declared, "I want to know Christ and the power of his resurrection" (Phil. 3:10 NIV).

The Savior offers His friendship to the human family. He opens Himself up to us, making Himself available. And Jesus Christ is very personal. He goes further than simply announcing from afar that He wants to have a personal relationship with us. "Here I am! I stand at the door and knock. If anyone hears my voice and opens the door, I will come in and eat with him, and he with me" (Rev. 3:20 NIV). My scholarly friend may use the term *sine qua non* here. The term simply means "that without which there is no other." Salvation is found in no one else, "for there is no other name under heaven given to men by which we must be saved" (Acts 4:12 NIV). Jesus says, "I am the gate; whoever enters through me will be saved" (John 10:9 NIV).

Jesus reminds us that heaven is not a meritocracy, a place where one is admitted on the basis of accomplishment. The kingdom about which Jesus speaks is a kingdom of grace. Only those who recognize their deep need, their utter helplessness without Christ, will find a place in this kingdom. When the religious teachers of Jesus' day theorized about the age to come, they were right in one sense. There will be a Messianic feast at the end of the age, but it will be Yahweh's feast, not ours. What a bitter disappointment it will be when the proud, those who thought they had a reserved seat at the table, suddenly realize that they are outsiders.

The problem with those on the outside is that they never really got to know Jesus. They never walked with Jesus, never had conversation with Him, never came to know what He likes and doesn't like. There was never really any intimacy between Jesus and them. This is what Jesus means when He says to the would-be elites, "I don't know you!" Yet more painful to these folk will be the sight of the very people they considered pagans, outcasts, even dogs, at the table with Abraham, Isaac, and Jacob. "There will be weeping and gnashing of teeth when you see Abraham and Isaac and Jacob and all the prophets in the kingdom of God, and you yourselves thrown out. Then people will come from east and west, from north and south, and will eat in the kingdom of God. Indeed, some are last who will be first, and some are first who will be last" (Luke 13:28-30 NIV).

The master-teacher sees the end from the beginning. At the outset He knows what will be important at the end of the day. Jesus knows what really counts. He sees in totality—past, present, and future.

My favorite Christian writer, Ellen White, states, "Christ's coming was at a time of intense worldliness. Men were subordinating the eternal to the temporal, the claims of the future to the affairs of the present. They were mistaking phantoms for realities, and realities for phantoms. They did not by faith behold the unseen world. Satan presented before them the things of this life as all-attractive and all-absorbing, and they gave heed to his temptations" (*Christ Object Lessons*, p. 26).

Jesus longs to break the spell. Jesus longs to free people who are really captive. He wants us to face up to realities. Friends, we are talking about the ultimate things when we talk about this future life, this banquet, and this perfect environment that are all in the Master's hands.

Those of us who profess to be on our way must keep in mind that it is Jesus's feast, and that it will take place at His house. Christ has sent out the invitations and He alone has the right to do this. He alone decides who comes. And He alone will provide the transportation to His place. "And if I go and prepare a place for you, I will come back and take you to be with me that you also may be where I am" (John 14:3 NIV). Everything about this grand and climactic event is in the hands of Jesus. He alone is sovereign Lord.

The sermon is ended. Jesus leaves us now to apply His words to our situation. The Word is always personal and relevant, searching us out, finding us, and conditioning us for salvation. It is ever good for what ails us.

THREE

Charles D. Brooks

Charles D. Brooks early distinguished himself as an erudite, eloquent speaker. Today, his diction and fluency with words are still cited as one of his draws. For the last thirty years of his ministry, Brooks was the speaker/director of the Breath of Life television program, an evangelistic endeavor that was the brainchild of Walter Arties, and a general field secretary of the General Conference of Seventh-day Adventists. Brooks is the darling of Christians who love a plain, uncompromising, no-holds-barred exposition of the Bible, and to date over 12,000 have been baptized as a result of his preaching. In addition, thirteen "Breath of Life" churches were established in the United States and overseas during his tenure as speaker/director of Breath of Life. Retired and living in Maryland, Brooks continues to serve as speaker emeritus of Breath of Life. In 1976, Brooks was named in *Who' Who in Religion*, and in *Notable Americans* in 1977. He was inducted into the Martin Luther King, Jr. Board of Preachers and Scholars at Morehouse College in Altanta, Georgia, in 1994.

The Interview

RCJ: Elder Brooks, when did preaching become an irresistible urge for you? How did you know you had been called to preach?

CDB: As a child, folk and family used to say to me, "That boy will be a preacher someday." I resisted the suggestion with all my heart. Graduating from high school in 1947, three close friends and I had decided to enter the pre-dentistry program an A&T University in our home city. Accepted into the program and with just two weeks to go before starting our first class, I was sitting all alone under the canvas pavilion of E. E. Cleveland's evangelistic crusade one Sabbath afternoon when God impressed me with the following words. "This is what I want you to do. I will help you to make truth clear." There was no audible voice, no bright light. It was just a profound impression that for the next several days returned with a strange power that made me both afraid and uncomfortable. When I told my mother, a saintly woman, about the experience she encouraged me to follow what she was sure was the voice of God. Immediately, I applied to Oakwood College to prepare to preach.

RCJ: Do you recall what you first preaching experience was like?

CDB: I had been at Oakwood for only a year and was home for the summer when our pastor stopped by to visit one day. "Charles, you're preparing to be a minister," he began, continuing with, "I want you to preach your first sermon while I am here as pastor." I was scheduled to preach in a month and a half. Though I felt ill-prepared and a bit of an amateur, I shall never forget my first sermon. The reason is that a brother who had left home when I was two and whom we had lost track of was in the audience that Sabbath morning. A family friend attending a party in New Jersey had stumbled upon my long-lost brother. The reunion that Sabbath was emotional, adding an element to my presentation that has been unforgettable.

RCJ: Who was your favorite preacher back then? Why? Did you have a mentor, someone who modeled preaching for you and whom you aspired to be like?

CDB: I've had several mentors over the years. My first pastor, N. B. Smith, was a veteran pastor who preached with power and conviction. Elder Smith was largely responsible for the spiritual tenor of our church because of the way he lived, taught, and treated people. My special inspiration came from E. E. Cleveland, a superlative exponent of truth. Cleveland preached in a powerful, incisive, and humble way that made people listen. He was especially effective in winning men. It was said of Cleveland (and later of me) that he always baptized an unusual proportion of men into the church. I don't know that I have ever tried to be like any preacher. What happens when I am in the pulpit is just me, that is, me greatly helped by God. Early in my ministry, though, I wanted to be patient like my father-in-law who could fearlessly combat injustice and meanness without allowing them to get the better of him.

RCJ: How do you define preaching? What is a sermon? And what is your theology of preaching?

CDB: One night as a group of us were sitting in the college barber shop at Oakwood, Dr. Frank L. Petersen, the college president, walked in. Excited that he was meeting with us on this level, a student asked him: "Sir, how do you prepare a sermon?" I shall never forget Petersen's answer. "Have an experience and then tell it," he said cryptically. How profound! Someone has said that a sermon is an excuse to talk about Jesus. It is an opportunity to define righteousness, to interpret the signs of the times, to clarify spiritual enigmas, to preach hope, and to call sinners to Christ and saints to faithfulness. My theology of preaching is basically to exalt Christ and His Word. Preachers must refrain from performing and seek to move people to Christ. We preachers have been called to preach only the Truth as it is found in Jesus. We are to lift up Christ as the only means and proof of salvation. A preacher ought to know God and God's word. I agree with Martin Luther who said: "One text of Scripture is worth more than a whole sermon." Because of my special call to do evangelism, I developed a way of making spiritual propositions and validating them with what is clearly presented in the Bible.

RCJ: Please share how you tackle the task of sermon preparation. Explain your step-by-step approach/method. How much reading do you do? Which commentaries do you consult? Where do you look for sermon illustrations? How many hours of preparation do you put into the average sermon? And how do you know a sermon is ready to be preached?

CDB: Since 1962, I have been a traveling minister who has had to deal with all the inconveniences, distractions and deprivations which come with that kind of ministry. In more ideal times (when I pastored churches), I had to prepare as many as three sermons a week. For my own benefit, I thought of them this way: Sabbath sermons were to be pastoral, Sunday night's were to be evangelistic, and those for Wednesday nights were to deal with things like modeling Jesus and Christian standards, etc. The subjects for these sermons usually came by inspiration, which involved prayer, Bible study, and reading, and preparation time varied from a few hours to several weeks. Elder Moseley, our beloved homiletics teacher at Oakwood, admonished us to carry notebooks for jotting down sermon thoughts and ideas. I've done that. A lot of my sermon illustrations have come straight out of the Bible, which I think is the best source for such material. Bible biographies and experiences are excellent examples for today's world. Newspapers also offer good illustrative material. Once the Lord and I have worked together on a sermon, I know it is ready to be preached. Yet I need to add an important point here. Sometimes a sermon you feel is just right may not go as well as one you do not feel as secure about. I believe, though, that all sermons bear fruit, even if the fruit is not immediately apparent.

RCJ: What kind of preacher are you? Topical, textual, or narrative?

CDB: I consider myself to be all three. I enjoy the variety, and am at ease with whichever the Spirit directs me to utilize.

RCJ: Do you write out your sermons? Do you preach from an outline, a manuscript, or are you an extemporaneous preacher? What

difference do you think outline, manuscript, or extemporaneous preaching makes?

CDB: Although I am able to preach without notes, I usually write out my sermons for several reasons. First, I want to stay within a time frame. Like most preachers, I am tempted to explore "tangential thoughts" that bombard the mind while one is preaching. Another reason I write out my sermons is so that I may familiarize myself with the material before the preaching event. Let me add that I enjoy listening to extemporaneous preaching as long as the preacher remains focused and coherent.

RCJ: Do you rehearse your sermons, preaching them out loud before actually delivering them?

CDB: No. I do not rehearse my sermons by preaching them out loud. I do, however, read through my material more than once as a rule. As I do so, I try to "see" the audience and anticipate the reactions of the people.

RCJ: How do you make the distant past of Scripture relevant to your listeners? What do you do to stay in touch with the contemporary world?

CDB: I believe the Bible is a living organ that is utterly contemporary. When I read the experiences of people like Joseph, the Hebrew worthies, Ezekiel, and Isaiah, I am transported back in time. Using words to paint pictures, I am able to transport my audience back to that time, as well as make the events and personalities of that time truly relevant to the experiences of my audience. Some preachers are more gifted at this than others.

RCJ: How important to preaching effectively is sitting silently before God to hear from God? How much time do you spend in so doing?

CDB: I believe that quiet meditation is vital to spiritual growth and life, and Scripture admonishes us to spend time this way. It was thus that Enoch "walked with God". I enjoy spending time with the Lord, although I am unable to quantify the amount of time I spend with God.

RCJ: Which person, experience, book, and commentary have had the greatest impact on your preaching?

CDB: When I was about six years old, *The Great Controversy* by Ellen G. White was brought to our home. I have often said that if I were marooned on a desert island and could have just three books I would choose the Bible, *The Great Controversy*, and *The Desire of Ages*, also by E. G. White. I could preach from these three books until Jesus comes. Believe it or not, my godly Mother, who now sleeps in Jesus, is the person who has had the most profound impact on my preaching. When I was about six months old God appeared to her as she laid on a hospital bed and told her that she should keep God's commandments. When she asked the Lord which one she was not keeping, she was shown the fourth commandment. My mother lived to see me ordained to the Seventh-day Adventist gospel ministry, and I think of her every time I enter the baptistry to baptize someone. I am, by grace, an extension of my mother's ministry. After her, Elders E. E. Cleveland and C. E. Moseley impacted my preaching the most.

RCJ: Do you think that any part of a sermon is more important than another? If you do, which do you think is the most important part?

CDB: Yes and no. Years ago, Elder Moseley taught us that each part of the sermon is important. If I had to single out a part, I would say it is the appeal. In the appeal the preacher must talk about Jesus, His blood, His matchless love, and His desire to save. The appeal must be emotional, but not purely or completely emotional. The emotions must drive the intellect to decide. Early in my ministry I preached a sermon I felt the Lord had attended with power. Yet I made no appeal. After the service a woman, with tears in her eyes, ran to me and said, "After hearing this message I must join this church. Why didn't you let me? Why didn't you give an invitation?" The valuable lesson I learned that day is that preachers must always make an appeal. I am never embarrassed if no one responds, believing that the response or lack of one is up to the Lord, not me.

RCJ: Can a preacher hit a "home run" every time he or she steps into the pulpit? And how do you bounce back from a bad sermon/day?

CDB: This interesting question speaks to the issue of how one measures a sermon. I believe that any sermon that a convicted minister prays over and labors with before God is a good sermon. Now it may not be what the people want, but I am sure it will be what they need. I also believe that preachers must strive to be faithful, not great. Once I suffered a severe bout of laryngitis as I was preaching to an audience of 30,000. What an awful experience it was! Because early in my preaching ministry I learned how to pray and preach simultaneously, I began to talk to God as I struggled with my delivery. I guess you would have to classify that sermon as a bad sermon. Yet afterwards many people told me that my physical condition made them listen more attentively. A gentleman told me that to this day he still weeps every time he listens to a tape of that sermon. So, a preacher can hit a "home run" each time he or she seeks to glorify God, has prayed and is prepared, and remains humble.

RCJ: How have you prevented your confidence from degenerating into cockiness? Conversely, how may the timid or fainthearted become more confident in the pulpit?

CDB: The key is knowing yourself. It is a false modesty that always presents the preacher as unworthy, ungifted, or unable to fulfill the preaching obligation. If you deny your gifts, how can you give the glory to God for them? Preachers must always thank God for the privilege to preach, remembering that God doesn't need them. God never has! We are preachers because of the grace and mercy of God. The gospel was preached quite well before I became a preacher and will be long after I am gone. That thought keeps me humble.

RCJ: Why do you think you are considered an outstanding preacher? What makes you effective? And how would you like to be remembered as a preacher?

CDB: I've never thought of myself as an outstanding preacher. I do not even have to resist those thoughts. Sermons I have preached may have been outstanding, but it was not because of any special eloquence or ability on my part. I simply preach the word of God. I have never given as much as five minutes to the study of style in my entire preaching ministry. When I get up there, it's just God and me. I do know I was called, and every person who preaches should be clear on this point. Knowing for sure that you have been called is an anchor. I may not be the most talented, but God called me; I may not be the best looking, but God called me; I may not be the most charismatic, but God called me. God called me.

RCJ: Do you follow a sermonic calendar? If not, how do you go about deciding what to preach from week to week?

CDB: I believe in the "cycle of truth," as inspiration calls it. I believe there are certain truths which ought to be repeated ever so often (Sabbath, Judgment, Second Coming, Christian Standards, etc.). I've always wanted to include special days to honor special people—the aged, youth, non-churched neighbors, etc.

RCJ: What is it you want your listeners to get out of your messages?

CDB: I want my listeners to hear the voice of God through His Word and my message calling them to higher, holier living. I want them to see Jesus, experience His love, and know of His unspeakable desire to save them. I want them to see and know that true joy comes when one walks with God. I want them to hear that God is a holy God and that those who are planning to live with God forever must themselves be a holy people.

RCJ: What do you think preaching will be like as we move further into the 21st century?

CDB: I do not like what I have been seeing. I think in the Adventist church we are getting more and more into neo-pentecostalism and "general" preaching. I have great confidence, however, that God is going to make serious adjustments and lead us back, as God promised, to primitive godliness. Jesus is coming soon, and He is coming for a peculiar people who are without spot or wrinkle. Right now, Jesus is competing for our attention. We should be preaching the three angels' messages, which is righteousness by faith in verity.

RCJ: What advice do you have for young preachers? What are some of the pitfalls to avoid, and the practices and disciplines to cultivate?

CDB: Young preachers, you are precious in God's sight and germane to God's program. Do not fail God. Get to know God and Jesus Christ, God's Sent One. Learn to pray, meditate, and study. Do not be deceived by some of the methods of TV preachers, and be leery of calling every kind of excitement the moving of the Holy Spirit. Study what you are preaching until you know it well and have been transformed by it yourself. Do not try to be popular, and avoid the traps of "filthy lucre" and "the flesh". Be a good husband or wife, knowing love as a principle. The torch is now in your hands. Please do not fail us

The Sermon

"A Controlled Burn"

The great day of the Lord is near—near and coming quickly. Listen! The cry on the day of the Lord will be bitter, the shouting of the warrior there. That day will be a day of wrath, a day of distress and anguish, a day of trouble and ruin, a day of darkness and gloom, a day of clouds and blackness, a day of trumpet and battle cry against the fortified cities and against the corner towers. I will bring distress on the people and they will walk like blind men, because they have sinned against the Lord. Their blood will be poured out like dust and their entrails like filth. Neither their silver nor their gold will be able to save them on the day of the Lord's wrath. In the fire of his jealously the whole world will be consumed, for he will make a sudden end of all who live in the earth" (Zeph. 1:14-18 NIV).

Huge fires are commonplace out west. Each year, millions of acres are burned over and burned out. In 1988, the biggest fire in recorded United States history raged in Yellowstone Park. In all, 150,00 acres were devastated. A reported later said, "It looked like hell had blown open!" On a sunny day at 3 p.m. it appeared like midnight, and only a heavy snow storm in mid-September could finally put out the fire.

In 2002, there was a terrible fire in Yosemite National Park. As I watched the report of the fire on the news, I saw a strange sight—men with torches spewing a jelled fuel were themselves setting fires. What in the world was going on?

There is an American treasure in Yosemite—the Sequoias, the biggest and tallest trees on earth. Some of these giant trees date back to the time of Christ. Fires have not been able to destroy these trees. Now, fires can kill harmful insects and disease. Fires can get rid of unsightly trees. Fires can annihilate trash and debris. But not these trees.

Because some trees carry their seeds in their crowns, fires cause them to pop open, releasing their kind of new life seedlings. So they do what is called a "controlled burn." Fires are deliberately set and controlled to destroy what may be destroyed and to release what is desirable.

Daniel 12 speaks of a "time of trouble" that is to come upon the earth just prior to the deliverance of the saints who "are found written in the book." Ellen White states that her pen could not describe this awful time, and many prophets, looking down the stream of the centuries to our day, could only exclaim, "My Lord!" One even cautioned about the day of the Lord. (See Amos 5:18-20).

As we contemplate these eventualities, we must fasten our faith on God's promises. "Lo, I am with you always, even to the consummation of the ages" (Matt. 28:2o). "God is faithful, who will not suffer you to be tempted above that ye are able" (1 Cor. 10:13). "When thou goest into the waters . . . and the fire . . . I will be with you" (Isa. 43:1-2). And the writer to the Hebrews tells us to "despise not the chastening of the Lord! Whom the Lord loveth, He chastens."

God allows the heat of tribulation that our earthliness might be consumed. Notice that it is our worldliness. We must deal with this early in our relationship with God. Earthliness deals with intrinsic weaknesses transmitted through DNA from Adam. Too much of this earth has rubbed off on us!

Catastrophes by land and sea, and fires, floods, and earthquakes are all in the forecast. They will be more frequent and more disastrous as time moves on. They will not be sent to destroy humanity en masse, but to wake us up. We see these signs now being fulfilled in our day. But the worst is yet to come, and all will culminate in the seven last plagues of Revelation 16.

Thank God for the hope of His Word. According to the psalmist, God will give His angels charge over us. No evil will befall us, even as thousands upon thousands fall by our sides.

Talk about security! The God who watches over us does not slumber or sleep (Psalm 121:4).

But there will be pressures, suffering, fear, and temptations. Yet these realities are God's agents to get us ready for a new neighborhood where our associates will be angels and in which we shall see God for ourselves. So much holiness will be required to get there that we are told that Jesus will be coming for a church without any defilement, without a spot or wrinkle or any such thing. When clothes are soiled, a good detergent will remove the spots, but the clothes are not yet ready to wear. The wrinkles must be removed. The most effective method of removing wrinkles is heat!

Ellen White writes: "The fact that we are called upon to endure trials shows that the Lord sees in us something precious which He desires to develop. If he saw nothing, He would not spend time refining us. . . . He does not cast worthless stones into His furnace" (*The Ministry of Healing*, p. 471).

What is usually our response to the refining process? We cry! We whine! We murmur and we complain! We lapse into our "pity party" mode, complaining, "Oh, dear me." When it's me, it's always dear. When, however, it is another dear soul who is going through trials and tribulations, we often conclude that because they made their bed they ought to lie in it. Once, somebody called me to say that they were angry with the Lord. I had to caution her that her accusation bordered on blasphemy, and, at the very least, was evidence of a lack of faith. In the midst of unspeakable misery Job was able to declare that if even God slew him he would continue trusting God. Friends, we must remember that what we are going through is a controlled burn. God's hand is on the thermostat.

A beautiful woman in prison was baptized through our prison ministry. She became strong in the Word of God, so much so that we put her in charge of the sixteen women who wanted Bible studies in jail. With no warning, the leader of this new group of women was informed that her laundry day was being switched to Saturday. What did she do? Boldly, she informed her officers that she could not violate the Sabbath and she pleaded for a change. I told her that this was only a test, a controlled burn. What do you know? A fellow inmate offered to switch days with her.

The Bible speaks of the time of Jacob's trouble which shall be a trial for God's people. Jacob had cheated his brother, Esau, deceived his father, and fled for his life. During a vision/dream, he saw a ladder reaching up to heaven. It was then that God renewed His covenant with the undeserving Jacob, who built an altar which he called Bethel. The spot was the "house of God and the gate to heaven."

Jacob went on to Mesopotamia, where he spent years in the employ of his unscrupulous kinsman (and father-in-law). Finally, he determined he should return to his home to receive the benefits of his birthright. Taking off for home, he led a huge entourage of servants, shepherds, and family. Together they provided evidence of God's blessings and Jacob's wealth. On the way, someone informed Jacob that his brother Esau was approaching with an army.

Jacob was devastated. He divided his group in the hope that some would survive. Then he stepped across the brook, Jabbok, and started to pray. This, he must do alone. We can never imagine the distress of Jacob. Notice that Esau hadn't even as much as laid a hand on him yet. In fact, Jacob hadn't even seen Esau. Why all this distress then? Why all this trouble?

Jacob had been obsessed by the power and promise of Bethel. He had believed God and worked all those years because he expected God's promise to be fulfilled. Now, it seems that God's word would not come true. Had he believed in vain? Had he been mislead? Had he misunderstood? Had the promises been directed to somebody else? Jacob was shaken to his bones. All he could think about was prayer—just himself and God! This was Jacob's trouble.

For you and me the questions will be: Am I really in the truth? Is obedience necessary? Is the Spirit of Prophecy dependable? Are the new and devisive things real or are they just a deception? Are the liberals right? And what about the conservatives? Some things will have to be settled. We must wrestle with God. We must review God's word until we overcome.

This experience was ultimate terrorism for Jacob. It seemed to him that he had been set up by another in the darkness of the night. Jacob didn't know who his antagonist was. Not until he had been touched and crippled by the person did Jacob know that it was the angel of God. The painful touch was his glorious epiphany!

Of this experience Ellen White says that Jacob knew it was God. Jacob knew God was merciful so he cast himself on that mercy. As Jacob looked at his life, he was brought to despair but he held fast with earnest, agonizing cries until he prevailed. This was a controlled burn, and such will be the experience of God's people in their final struggle with the powers of evil. God will test our faith, our perseverance, and our confidence in His power to deliver us, and we must not let go because our prayers are not immediately answered. Ellen White says that Jacob's experience is an assurance that God will not cast off those who have been betrayed into sin, but who have returned to Him in true repentance. (*Patriarchs and Prophets*, p. 177).

I lost my last and favorite brother. He was diagnosed with cancer and was dead in seven weeks. When I was free on Sabbaths, I drove hundreds of miles to visit him. When I was engaged, I called. Once, when I called from Los Angeles, I was greeted by some really bad news. Able to detect that I was greatly affected, my brother said, "Chuck, even if God doesn't heal me, look where I'm headed." He then began to talk about the coming of Jesus, the resurrection of the righteous, the ascension, and the reunion in heaven. Our souls will be lifted up there. There'll be no more sickness or sorrow there. When I was asked to deliver my brother's eulogy, I chose as my title, "Look Where I'm Headed."

God's servants have always suffered. Jesus said, "The world will hate you." Does Jesus tell the truth. Jesus does not offer riches or relief from suffering. He Himself was opposed by the forces of evil. Satan has persecuted and put to death God's people in all ages. Yet in dying God's people have become more than conquerors.

We must walk narrow paths on earth, where God will refine us as gold is refined and purify us as silver is purified. And God will continue to do this until we learn to look at sin with abhorrence. The apostle Paul declared: "I reckon that the sufferings of the present are not worthy to be compared with the glory which will be revealed" (Rom. 8:18).

God is planning one humongous celebration for us when we get home. I read somewhere that one glimpse, not one week end or one month's vacation there, of what God is preparing for us will cause us to view the trials and sufferings of this world as nothing. Dr. Martin Luther King, Jr. said that his greatest trial was in overcoming the fear of death. On the last night of his life he proclaimed a victory over that fear. That is a victory that we as Christians must claim and experience, too.

A young woman joined the church one day after my sermon. She went home to tell her live-in boyfriend that she had made a commitment to Christ. He was furious, especially after learning that if he did not marry her he would have to move out. The boyfriend's anger escalated until he pulled out a revolver and scattered her brains on the floor one day. As the local church pastor and I related the tragic new to the congregation, we were both in tears. Then it dawned on us. The sound of an explosion was probably the last thing she had heard. The next sound she will hear will be the penetrating peal of a trumpet calling her from the tomb. Her next sight will be that of Jesus coming in matchless glory, and the next sensation she will feel will be that of rising up to meet Jesus in the air. She will be drawn by the irresistible power of her sovereign King and His love. She will be so superbly happy and ecstatically thrilled that she will pass off her last memory and anger and confusion in this world as simply "A Controlled Burn."

Jesus promised that He will come quickly. He is soon to appear. The signs are everywhere. Jesus is coming again.

FOUR

Edward Earl Cleveland

Edward Earl Cleveland was the first Seventh-day Adventist preacher to baptize 1,000 people in an evangelistic campaign. Now retired after over fifty-five years in the gospel ministry, Cleveland lives in Huntsville, Alabama, where he serves as an adjunct professor in the Department of Theology and Religion at Oakwood College, his alma mater. Before his retirement, Cleveland was unarguably Adventism's premiere evangelist, redefining evangelism and rewriting the denomination's evangelism manual. Today, Cleveland is one of the most widely recognized Seventh-day Adventist personalities, and continues to serve as a contributor for *Message Magazine*. Known for his "holy boldness" in the pulpit, Cleveland mastered the art of the altar call, succeeding in baptizing over 16,000 people as a result. Through it all, Cleveland still found time to author fourteen books and two Adult Sabbath School Lesson Quarterlies (1964 and 1981). Cleveland has been listed in *Who's Who in Black America*, *Who's Who in Religion in America*, and *Men of Achievement*. He was inducted into the Martin Luther King, Jr. Board of Preachers and Scholars at Morehouse College in Atlanta, Georgia, in 1993. His sermon, "These Things," is a reprint of a sermon first published in the July 11, 2002 issue of the *Adventist Review*.

The Interview

RCJ: Elder Cleveland, when and how did you know God had definitely called you to preach?

EEC: I believe a person is called to preach by three methods—original conviction, association, and direct confrontation. For me, it was conviction, as was the case with Samuel. My earliest ambition was to be a preacher, to populate the Kingdom of God. My father used to take me to evangelistic crusades when my feet barely touched the saw dust, and I listened to preachers like G. E. Peters and F. L. Peterson. I think my father wanted me to be an evangelist. He was the father of three boys and a member of the Georgia-Cumberland Conference Committee who served as an elder for approximately forty-five years. The brethren wanted to give him a district to pastor, but he respectfully declined, telling them that he would give his three sons to the service of God instead. I have always wanted to be an evangelist, never having any interest in pastoring. I pastored seven years and longed for deliverance. When I was made conference evangelist in my eight year of ministry, I started singing "Free at Last".

RCJ: In addition to the individuals you just mentioned, who were the preachers that had an impact on you during your formative years? Who were the preachers to whom you looked for inspiration and guidance?

EEC: Nobody could attend Oakwood during my time, that is from the late 30's through the mid-40s, and not be influenced by C. E. Moseley. Now, I was not one of his favorite students, the reason being that we were too much alike. Because I was a student of the Word from my childhood, I wasn't too sure that anybody could teach me anything about the Bible. Moseley and I were always bumping heads, in part because I was not intimidated by him as were the other students. Once I even openly challenged him about an examination question. I guess I was somewhat immature. I never realized the error of my ways until I graduated without a call. H. L. Singleton was another person whom I greatly admired. I'll say more about him later.

RCJ: Why exactly did you admire about C. E. Moseley and H. L. Singleton?

EEC: I admired Moseley because of his keen mind and powerful preaching, and Singleton because when I was finally hired it was to him I was assigned. Singleton was a stickler for methodology, and even though he was not a powerful preacher, he had the ability to persuade people. Singleton taught me soul winning. When he got through with me, I had several small index cards with nothing but Singletonology written on them.

RCJ: Do you recall what your first sermon was like?

EEC: I'll never forget it. I was summoned to Charlotte, North Carolina, by the conference president, a wonderful German I expect to meet in heaven because he hired me after I had been in the wilderness with no prospect of being hired for over a year. I was placed on a chair in the middle of a room of five white men who interrogated me as if they were the FBI and I was America's most wanted. After the interrogation, I was told I would preach the following day at the colored church. My title was, "Can a Man be Perfect?" I was preaching for my life. All the conference brethren were present, and later I was made to understand that they really didn't want to hire me.

Fifteen minutes into the sermon the Negroes were shouting, the white women were dabbing at their eyes, and everybody was trying to control themselves.

RCJ: What do you think accounted for the reaction of your audience?

EEC: It had to be the Holy Ghost. It was not because the sermon was deep or preached with power. I was literally caught away in the Spirit. I cannot recall if my theology was correct that day, but I can state firmly that the Lord took my crumbs and multiplied them. When the conference president returned to his conference committee, he stated that he would only entertain one name for a pastoral internship—mine! "Can a Man be Perfect?" is definitely the most memorable sermon I have ever preached, and I have preached in front of some pretty important people across the earth.

RCJ: Did you start preaching as an adult?

EEC: Oh no. I've been preaching since I was five. My father used to write out little sermons for me and I would memorize them as a five-year-old. Then dad would drive me around to "First Day Churches" where I'd preached my little heart out. Strangely, my father never complimented me. So one day I asked, "Daddy, was it alright?" "Well son," he replied, "you still have a lot of rough edges, a lot of rough edges, to work on." That's the most in the way of a compliment about my preaching that I ever got from him.

RCJ: I'm sure he was proud of your later success.

EEC: I used to invite my father to help me baptize folk years later. Once, after we had baptized so many people that his arm ached, I asked him: "Dad, how was the day?" Looking up from his meal he replied that the day was pretty good but that it was less than what I could have done, and he returned to eating. His attitude toward me as a preacher made me afraid of myself, and I didn't understand it until I picked through *The Desire of Ages* and read where Ellen White said some things about the popularity and power of John the Baptist that helped me tremendously.

RCJ: How would you assess your preaching? What is it that makes you effective?

EEC: First, realizing that I am not as effective as I ought to be or want to be. As a preacher yourself, you well know that preachers are seldom, if ever, satisfied with a presentation they make. I depend on the Holy Spirit totally. There is a little saying I use all the time that goes like this, "I have seen God do so much for so long with so little, that I now believe God can do anything with nothing, meaning me."

RCJ: How do you keep your self-confidence from slipping into arrogance?

EEC: Interestingly, there are some people who think I am arrogant. I am not. Learning to differentiate between arrogance and Spirit-inspired boldness is something some preachers have to learn, but I am not one of those. The Bible says that the early apostles spoke with great boldness. Take Peter, for example. After Pentecost, Peter was not a running coward. Some years ago a young lady in Louisville, Kentucky told me that at one time she had thought I was arrogant, but that she had come to view what she thought as arrogance as holy boldness.

RCJ: How do you bounce back from a bad sermon?

EEC: I'll never forget a sermon I preached at the old Shiloh church in Chicago. It was preached on a Sunday night and Elder Kibble, the conference president, was present. My subject was the mark of the beast, and I wasn't much into the sermon when I knew that I was struggling. I was glad to finish the sermon and sat down without making an appeal. I was discouraged, and in bad shape. I was sure nobody would join the church on that sermon.

RCJ: What happened next?

EEC: Elder Kibble rose and announced the closing song. While we were singing a man came running down the aisle. Leaning over from the rostrum, Kibble gave the man his ear. I was surprised when the conference president whispered to me: " This man is trying to join the church. What shall I do?" I told Elder Kibble to step back and I took over. The lesson I learned that night is that we are bad judges of sermons. I've seen five, six, seven, and eight people accept Jesus as their Savior in response to sermons that would never meet the minimum standards of a good sermon. I think the Lord allows that to happen to teach us our utter dependency on Him. It is so easy to go to bed humble and wake up like Nebuchadnezzar saying, "Isn't this great Babylon that I have built?" I was asked once to share the secret of my success and I responded that the secret of my success is that I have not yet succeeded. I wasn't playing, either.

RCJ: Talking about the secret of your success, what is the secret of a successful appeal. Many people believe you have the gift of appeal, and that your ability to get people "over the line" is unmatched. I have listened to you on several occasions and cannot recall you ever "opening the doors of the church" and people not responding. In fact, sometimes you ask people seated down front to vacate the pews so that those coming forward will have a place to sit. The vacated pews never remain empty. What makes you so sure that people will always respond positively to your appeals?

EEC: Let me take you back to my tent meetings. One thing that enabled me to begin to baptize hundreds was what I noticed with Singleton. I noted that Singleton in his sermons would ask everybody who planned to go all the way with the Lord to meet him at the piano, organ, or somewhere else. Invariably, there were fifteen, twenty, or twenty-five people at the appointed place waiting for him. Yet I couldn't understand why Singleton would split his congregation, so I resolved to do things a little differently. I started keeping everybody together and telling them that the next Sabbath there was going to be a big baptism. I informed the women, as well as the men, what they had to place in their baptism bags, and encouraged them to bring their bundles to the meetings before the Sabbath. I was the one who started the bundle collection plan. In the meantime, Bible instructors visited them. The result was that I always had a decent baptism.

RCJ: What about your pew-clearing strategy?

EEC: Well, I evolved to the point where I have no fear of clearing benches, and sometimes four or five pews will fill up. Getting people to come forward is based on a sure thing that God hit me with one day. God revealed to me that every time I preach there are three classes of people before me, and that I should ask them to come forward all at the same time.

RCJ: Tell me about the three classes of people.

EEC: First are former Seventh-day Adventists whose walk with the Lord has soured. I ask them to come in out of the rain, to come back to Jesus and experience true happiness again. The second group consists of Christians of other faiths who for a long time have wanted to join the Adventist church. I call on them not to put it off any longer. Then there is the third class of people. This group consists of people who have never experienced conversion until that day. I describe conversion for these folk, so that they know what they have just experienced is conversion. After describing each group, I ask those to whom the description applies not to move until the congregation begins to sing "Pass me not, O gentle Savior." I am very bold about it.

RCJ: So you have to be bold?

EEC: Yes, you have to be. You have to believe in what you are saying and know that God is attending your efforts. It is not always easy though. Sometimes you have to wait awhile before anybody moves. Once, in Denver, nobody moved after I had been appealing for five minutes. I then told the congregation that I was an old fisherman looking for souls for the Master's kingdom, and that my years of fishing were telling me that there were fishes there. I invited the congregation to sing the first stanza of our appeal song again, and, lo and behold, people started coming forward. I think we filled up three pews that day.

RCJ: Have you ever made an appeal to which no one responded positively?

EEC: Not in my fifty-nine years of preaching. And that holds true if we include the time when I was learning the craft. I don't see how a preacher can come up dry if the Lord is with him or her. I once baptized thirteen people in Durham, North Carolina, and thought that I had lost it. I went out to the woods before moving on to Greensboro, North Carolina, and told the Lord that I could not live with thirteen baptisms. I informed God that I wanted 100. One of my interns in that crusade in Greensboro was Eric Ward. I told him, "Don't worry, son. This one is in the bag." At the end of twelve weeks we baptized 114 people. From then on it's been hundreds, hundreds, hundreds. But I had to settle it with God personally.

RCJ: How much time do you spend talking with God in preparation for preaching?

EEC: Well, I follow the Scripture that call on us to pray without ceasing. I go over three passages of Scripture every morning, and this morning was no exception. The first is 2 Samuel 7:8; the second is Nehemiah 13:14; and the third is Exodus 23:25. With 2 Samuel 7:8, I simply replace David's name with mine. God told David he took him from following his daddy's sheep and made him a king over Israel. I remind myself that it is God who made me whatever I am. God took me from pushing carts selling ice cream and other stuff for my father and gave me a name. I never ran a meeting in which I did not ask the Lord to remember me, as did Nehemiah in Nehemiah 13:14. I claim the promises of God with Exodus 23:25. When I was told I had prostrate cancer, the prognosis, from a medical standpoint, did not look good. Loma Linda told me that they could not heal me. I told them that they were correct. They could treat me, but they could not heal me. I informed them I would deal with the Healer myself. And so, I have been living with the vitamins from those three passages of Scripture for years now.

RCJ: In your almost-sixty years of evangelistic preaching, you have seen and experienced many changes. What do you think is the future of evangelistic preaching?

EEC: Well, Mrs. White has given us two things. She talks about a lay movement developing for the future. She sees members going from home to home under very difficult circumstances and thousands joining the church under those conditions. During the four years that I had North America as my exclusive domain, I promoted what Mrs. White saw as the missing link in the Adventist chain. We have millions of lay people out there who regard baptism as a spectator sport and the preacher as a performer. I don't think that preaching will ever end as a means of bringing people to Christ, and I don't believe that public evangelism will ever come to an end. Just look at Mark Finley.

RCJ: Suppose you had to conduct a field school of evangelism next summer. Picture before you a room full of young, eager men and women interested in evangelistic preaching. What counsel or advice would you give to them?

EEC: First, I would remind them that there are Christians outside of our denomination. If they get that concept they will be kinder to even preachers of other faiths. The second thing I would tell them is to remember that they are Seventh-day Adventist preachers who are called to preach a distinctive message. People ought to know for sure that they are listening to an Adventist preacher, not someone from the Unitarian church across town. Listening to an Adventist preacher, they should hear something they won't hear anywhere else. Next, I would encourage an Adventist evangelistic preacher to wrestle with the question of righteousness by faith. People have got to know that it is the atoning act of Christ that clears us in the judgement and that it is our love for him and vice versa that enables us to stay in this relationship.

RCJ: Let's switch gears now. What is your understanding of black preaching? And do you think that Adventist preaching, with its distinctive ethos and focus on reform and doctrines, and black preaching are mutually exclusive?

EEC: To me, Adventist preaching and black preaching are totally compatible. Black preaching is more than an emotional message based on my experience. It is relating the reality of the gospel to the contextual struggle of black people and reassuring them that the God of the Hebrews is their God, too. God is a deliverance-minded deity. He proved this in His dealings with the Hebrews, and He has proven it to us. I believe that for anybody to do effective black preaching he or she must know black history. If not, the preacher will not even know to whom he or she is talking. It is for this reason that I think a course in black history must be included in the curriculum for all who hope to engage in black preaching.

RCJ: You have been preaching for approximately sisty years. How has preaching in general, and black SDA preaching in particular, changed over the years?

EEC: I haven't seen that much of a change in either. We have always emphasized Jesus. Take the subject of the sanctuary, for example. Most black SDA preachers have always stressed that the sanctuary is all about Jesus and the whole plan of salvation. What went on in the earthly sanctuary, things like the slaying of the lamb, the offering of the blood, and the judgement of the people, all pointed to Jesus. Other folk have allowed themselves to be caught up with all the paraphenilia, but not us. I was raised on Jesus first, last, and always.

RCJ: Can you explain what you mean?

EEC: Recently I was at a camp meeting at which Henry Wright preached. In his sermon, which I think was a masterpiece, Henry said, and I'm paraphrasing now: "Folks, I know some people are always kind of hung up on details and so forth, but I couldn't care less about how wide the Most Holy Place was, and I couldn't care less if there were no candlesticks in heaven." When I heard that I jumped up and hollered. Henry continued, "Look, in the judgment, it is the Lord and the atonement, the Lord and the crucifixion, the Lord and the resurrection, and the Lord and His priestly ministry. It is the Lord working for you and for me. Let us therefore come boldly before the throne of grace. Quit arguing about where the throne is. Is it in the Most Holy Place? Is it in the Holy Place? Did it move from the Holy Place to the Most Holy Place in 1844? You can argue all day, but let me tell you one thing. There is a throne, and He is there, and He told me when I need him to come to the throne and I'll find grace. Now, how many of you need some mercy, and how many of you need some grace?" Henry would have been happy to see me that night.

RCJ: So, it's all about Jesus?

EEC: Yes, and we cannot allow T. D. Jakes and Rod Parsley and others to rob us of that. Our prophet, who died almost a century ago, admonished us to preach Jesus Christ and we won't be as dry as the hills of Gilboa. We need to get more of Jesus into our sermons.

RCJ: How would you like to be remembered as a preacher?

EEC: I would like to be remembered as the person who made evangelism a living thing among Adventist preachers. My one ambition as a preacher has been to so advertise and represent evangelism, that no preacher would allow it to die. I want evangelism to always be something that is desired.

RCJ: I take it you always wanted to be an evangelist.

EEC: Once, the brethren were interested in my becoming president of one of our conferences. The outgoing president sat with me in a trailer on the campground until 3 a.m. one day trying to convince me that this was God's will for me. I declined. Why? Because I was interested in doing evangelism. When I was elected to the Ministerial Association of the General Conference, I was informed that I would not be doing any more evangelistic preaching; I'd just travel the world and teach other people how to do it. On hearing that I told the brethren that they had elected the wrong man. And just before I left the General Conference the brethren tried to make me a vice president of the General Conference. Again I declined. I had set my sight on being an evangelist, and wanted to die one. I also wanted to inspire pastoral productivity.

RCJ: Are there any preachers you are mentoring now? Anyone to whom you are teaching the science and art of evangelistic preaching?

EEC: People still call me from near and far. But I am not mentoring any single individual, per se, right now. I'll tell what excites me though. Nothing excites me more that sitting at a Workers' Meeting and hearing reports of public evangelism. I'm most happy when I hear that people are still pitching tents.

The Sermon

"These Things"

"And as he sat upon the mount of Olives, the disciples came unto him privately, saying, 'Tell us, when shall these things be?'" (Matt. 24:3).

As Jesus and His disciples departed from the Temple, they called His attention to the building's striking beauty. Standing in majestic splendor on what today is known as the Dome of the Rock, gleaming like a pearl kissed by the Judean sunlight, it was the centerpiece of Jewish pride and worship. But the disciples were stopped short in their verbal praise by the Master's startling response: "There shall not be left here one stone upon another, that shall not be thrown down" (Matt. 24:2).

The disciples could understand Christ's denunciation of the religious leaders that had just occurred, but this reference to the Temple was another matter. He must be talking about the end of the world, they mused. What else could eclipse the glory of the Temple or bring it down? And so they asked, "When shall these things be? And what shall be the sign . . .?" (verse 3).

In His response, Jesus addressed "these things" as end-time events as well as the end of the Temple shrine, considering the latter occurrence as the visible sign of the end of God's contract with Israel. It was Titus who in A.D. 70 led his screaming eagle legions against Jersualem and razed the Temple so *that not one stone was left upon another.*

Jesus continued His discourse, stressing the parallel signs that would transpire preceding the destruction of Jerusalem and the "end of the world": war and its attendant evils; famine, pestilence, and upheavals in nature (verses 6, 7); and the preaching of the gospel to the world (verse 14). The Scriptures indicate that this was accomplished in a limited way prior to the demise of the Temple (Rom. 1:5; Acts 17:6), and it is a thing in progress as we approach the coming of the Lord.

An Unpopular Message

The word that our era is hurtling toward its conclusion with consummate speed is not a popular message to bear. People would rather hear that the dead are in heaven, caught away to be with God. That the second coming of the Christ is a secret rapture thing. That the first day of the week has replaced the Sabbath as the true Lord's day. That the saints will be raptured before the great tribulation.

While people are being lulled to sleep by false prophets, the true gospel of the kingdom will be preached planet-wide "for a witness unto all nations; and then shall the end come" (Matt. 24:14). While spirits of devils are working miracles, and psychic hot lines spin their yarns, the rising tide of truth will flood the world. God has promised to raise up a people who will "teach my people the difference between the holy and the profane, and cause them to discern between the unclean and the clean" (Eze. 44:23). "They shall keep my laws and my statutes . . . and they shall hallow my sabbaths" (verse 24).

Yes, while the secret rapture theory flows freely from the lips of world-renowned clergy, the truth about the Second Coming will peal like thunder and strike like lightning. And what is that truth? "And then shall appear the sign of the Son of man in heaven: and then shall all tribes of the earth mourn, and they shall see the Son of man coming in the clouds of heaven with power and great glory" (Matt. 24:30). This scripture kills the secret rapture. They shall see His coming! Paul suggests in 1 Thessalonians 4:18 that we "comfort one another with these words." Matthew 24:14 fingers this preaching as a sign of the end.

In 2 Timothy 3:13 we find yet another sign of the end of human rule on this planet. "Evil men and seducers shall wax worse and worse." In the last days "perilous times shall come" (verse 1). Are they not here? In September 2001 we witnessed a criminal act that has spread terror through the world. The twin towers in New York were demolished by human hijackers in a frightening display of human wickedness, killing nearly 3,000 unsuspecting human beings. This dastardly deed and its ripple effects have closed industries, costing thousands of jobs. It was a scheme conceived in hell. There have been other crimes against humanity that should have been a wake-up call, but we slept on. Do you remember Hitler? Have you heard of Buchenwald, Dachau, Auschwitz, and Treblinka?

These signs of human bestiality have ushered us into a reign of terror that God will not long tolerate. "These things" shout in a language clear: Christ is coming soon! Meanwhile, terror reigns supreme worldwide. Our Lord predicted: "There shall be signs in the sun, and in the moon, and in the stars; and upon the earth distress of nations, with perplexity . . . men's hearts failing them for fear" (Luke 21:25, 26).

Consider the trouble spots: Palestine, Kashmir, Korea, the Balkans; and consider how terror stalks the rest of the world: the United States, Europe, Asia. Indeed, the world has come to feel its vulnerability. It seems that the froglike demons of Revelation 16 are on the move, spreading confusion and fear wherever their loathsome bodies land.

But there is good news. While fear riddles the human environment, genuine Christians manifest calm in the eye of the storm. We know that the days are evil and that life has reached a new level of danger. But the Christian knows something else: "God is our refuge and strength, a very present help in trouble. Therefore will not we fear, though the earth be removed" (Psalm 46:1, 2). "For God hath not given us the spirit of fear; but of power, and of love, and of a sound mind" (2 Tim. 1:7). And we are comforted by the upward look: "When these things begin to come to pass, then look up, and lift up your heads; for your redemption draweth nigh" (Luke 21: 28).

We do not know the day and the hour of His return. We do not need to. The Christian's word is not "when," but "whenever." We must be ready "whenever" He comes. Christians know their primary responsibility to this end-time generation—and that is to spread the good news to every person on earth.

Fulfilling the Great Sign Even Through Persecution

The supreme passion of the saints in all ages has been to share the "blessed hope." Troublesome times have been a stimulus, not a depressant. Under the mad Caesars, the decree went forth, "'Non-licet Esse Vos'— you have no right to exist." The bloody executions that followed merely strengthened the Christians' resolve to bear a faithful witness. As they awaited their turns in the death dens of the Roman Colosseum, their slogan was "Let's show these pagans how to die." Of themselves they could not manifest such courage. Nor could we.

The secret of such steadfastness is found in Scripture. "Fear thou not; for I am with thee; be not dismayed; for I am thy God; I will strengthen thee; yea, I will help thee; Yea, I will uphold thee with the right hand of my righteousness" (Isa. 41:10). "Go ye therefore, and teach all nations, . . . and, lo, I am with you alway, even unto the end of the world" (Matt. 28:19, 20). Their faith in these promises was tested by adversity, and they found in Christ a shock absorber. John Huss could sing hymns while flames cooked his flesh, for Christ was his painkiller. Paul could go willingly to Nero's chopping block because Christ is the resurrection! Christ in you makes *bearable* the *unbearable*.

Toward the Grand Climax

America has been perhaps the most successful experiment in human government in the history of the world, its imperfections notwithstanding. No nation before it has promised so much to so many. The crowned heads of Europe, including the pope, scoffed at the idea of a "kingdom without a king and a church without a pope." But the nation grew in wealth and influence until it became the leader of the free world. Its Christian missionaries are everywhere evident, operating schools, clinics, and hospitals, and feeding the hungry. In times of crisis American granaries have fed millions, and its treasure has secured the financial solvency of nations. However, America is not without its serious deficiencies, and the will to deal with these travels sometimes at the pace of a snail. The United States now stand at the pinnacle of its power—the most influential power since the fall of the Roman Empire. The attack on Pearl Harbor and that of September 11 shook its complacency.

Christians in America suffered with those who lost their lives on both occasions. Indeed, the pain still lingers. But while Christians experience pain with others, Christians are comforted by the redemptive event that these events signify—namely, the coming of our Lord, who will put an end to all such occurrences.

And even in America, as the Bible predicts, oppression rears its ugly head and we hear the serpent's hiss or the dragon's roar, it will merely quicken our pace and hasten our steps toward that better land "where the wicked cease from trouble and the weary are at rest."

FIVE

James Doggette

James Doggette teaches in the Department of Religion and Theology at Oakwood College, where he is powerfully impacting a new generation of Adventist preachers. Doggette also pastors the Madison Mission SDA Church in Decatur, Alabama, which he planted and today is one of the fastest growing churches in the Southern Union Conference of Seventh-day Adventists. Before joining the faculty of Oakwood, Doggette was the senior pastor of the Valley Fellowship SDA Church in southern California, where, as a direct consequence of his preaching, worship services were standing-room-only affairs. A charismatic, captivating preacher whose pulpit prowess makes him a favorite of young professionals, Doggette is known for his creativity, energy, passion, and imagery. His ability to make the truths of Scripture relevant to young professionals is unrivaled. Worship at the Madison SDA Church in general, and Doggette's preaching in particular, draw people from around the country. His style is interactive, and he seldom, if ever, preaches with notes.

The Interview

RCJ: Tell me something about who you are and what made you decide to be a preacher.

JD: I was born in Southern California and spent most of my life there, though my family did live in several parts of the United States, including the South. I'm the son of an Adventist preacher, the brother of an Adventist preacher, the nephew of a)n Adventist preacher, and the grandson of an Adventist preacher. My grandmother was an Adventist Bible worker, and my mother worked as a teacher in our school system. I guess you can say I'm a child of the church who felt called to the ministry from his earliest years.

RCJ: So, you were surrounded by Adventist preachers all your life, and they had a powerful impact on you.

JD: I know the children of some ministers end up resenting the church, but it is different with me. I feel blessed that my father was a minister who spent a lot of time with his children. The church did not rob us of a father; in fact, it added to our lives. It was my father's preaching that convinced me that I should be a preacher, too. I distinctly remember a sermon he preached when I was about 7 or 8. The title of the sermon was "How Great Thou Art," and one reason I can vividly recall the sermon is because dad was going through a storm at his church at the time. I remember my father, who was usually stoic and calm, crying as he preached about God and how great God is. There was something rather compelling about the experience, and I remember saying as I sat through it: "I want to do that. That's exactly what I want to do." It was an epiphanal moment for me.

RCJ: Your decision to be a preacher, then, was made in childhood, at about age 8?

JD: Yes, and it was largely due to the respect I had for my father. There were other ministers in my family, but I was drawn to my dad. I really wanted to be like him.

RCJ: Was there ever a time when you reconsidered your decision to be a preacher?

JD: Somewhere between my last year in high school and my first year in college I faltered somewhat. I didn't do too well my senior year in high school and needed to mature a bit before college, so I took a year off. During that year I decided I wanted to be an eye doctor, and because I did OK in the sciences on the SAT, I was recruited by the Science Department at Oakwood. I did well in the department, but I just did not feel at home there. After a semester, I transferred to the Religion and Theology Department, where I felt very much at home even though I did not do great in all my classes there. I was at peace with myself.

RCJ: Other than your father, who were the preachers to whom you were drawn, and why?

JD: There were a few of them. One was D. J. Williams, who did a Week of Prayer for my father once. D. J. preached a sermon about the second coming entitled "Moving Toward Daybreak" that was so compelling I thought he would explode. He was an animated preacher who held nothing back, and when he banged on the pulpit I thought it would break. What fascinated me about D. J. was how he totally lost himself in what he was doing and saying, and I remember saying to myself, "I want to do that." I even went home and tried to get my whoop on. Of course, I sounded rather silly.

RCJ: Who else influenced you?

JD: Another individual who gripped me fairly early was Billy Graham. I know it may sound strange for an African American preacher to say that he was influenced by Billy Graham, but I was. I never saw him live, only on television, but the thing that impressed me about him was his ability to hold the attention of the masses. The third person who influenced me as a young man was Barry Black, who worked as a tent master for my dad during one of my father's evangelistic crusades in Memphis, Tennessee. Barry was a real attraction, a real draw, at the meetings because he often did narrations of Dr. Martin Luther King, Jr's speeches. I was impressed by Barry's incredible memory and the ways in which he could use his voice. The day after my father preached about the state of the dead, Barry was able to preach the sermon to me, quoting my father almost word for word. To say I was fascinated by his memory is really to utter an understatement.

RCJ: Do you recall what your first preaching outing was like?

JD: The first sermon I delivered after making the decision to enter the pastoral ministry was at Oakwood College during my freshman year. Actually, I remember my first two sermons because they go together. My first sermon was about Elijah declaring, "It's Gonna Rain," when there were cloudless skies, and it was preached for a Freshman men's worship at Moran Hall. The response to the sermon was overwhelmingly positive and I interpreted that to mean I was a great preacher. As such, I couldn't wait to preach again and actually worked out another preaching engagement for the same venue. I was authentic the first time around, just talking the way I talk, but I decided that for my second sermon I would growl. I would do the D. J. Williams thing. I was so confident I invited half the campus to come to hear me that night, including my older brother, who was a senior, and Henry Wright, a homiletical genius.

RCJ: How did the sermon turn out?

JD: My text was from Mark, where it says that Jesus went into a house and would have no man know it, but He could not be hid, and my one little idea was that when Jesus is on the inside, it can't be hid. It's going to be obvious by the things you do. I had absolutely no development of that one idea; I simply knew that I was going to holler that idea. As soon as I prayed, I started screaming uncontrollably. Everyone, including me, knew that I was out of control. How well do I remember the expressions on people's faces. My brother, eyebrows raised, had a bewildered expression on his face, as if asking, "What's going on?" I screamed until, mouth dry, I had nothing else to say, and finally slumped down into my chair. I was so humiliated I wanted the floor to open up and swallow me. It was an awful feeling that I never want to experience again.

64 PREACHING WITH POWER

RCJ: What did you learn from the experience?

JD: I learned a much-needed lesson in humility. I learned never to enter the pulpit confident in your own ability. I learned that preaching is sort of like the mechanical rabbit that runs in front of the greyhound. It doesn't matter how well you run, you're not going to catch it. Preaching is always something to which you'll be reaching out, and even if your sermon is wonderful, it will not be perfect. Preachers are ever in the process of trying to get there.

RCJ: What's your definition of preaching?

JD: To me, the best definition I've ever read is Brooks' definition of preaching as truth poured out through personality. My definition and understanding of preaching is similar to that. Preaching is divine truth or biblical truth communicated through a personality. I do not believe that preaching is merely verbal communication, but an event, an experience that goes beyond the spoken words. I believe divine truth can be communicated in many different ways, but only people can preach because only people possess personality. A preacher who tries to hide his or her personality will never be an effective preacher.

RCJ: What about black preaching? How do you define black preaching?

JD: More than anything, black preaching is prophetic. The central content of black preaching today is akin to that of the prophets of the Old Testament. That central message is that everything is not alright in our world, and that even though God is ultimately going to bring about a reversal of the social order, those in power should curb their ways and attitudes toward the poor and voiceless. This is what the prophet Isaiah is essentially declaring in Isaiah 58 and 59. The black preacher is always walking up to those in power, waving his or her finger in front of their noses, and saying, "Use the power you have right because God is ultimately going to cast down those who are using power unjustly." Now that was clearly the content of Jesus' preaching, too, as is evidenced in Jesus' Sermon on the Mount.

RCJ: As Adventists, we place a lot of emphasis on doctrine, prophecy, and reform, leading some to conclude that Adventist preaching and black preaching are mutually exclusive. Do you agree or disagree?

JD: I think I am authentically black and authentically Adventist in my presentations, although I would hasten to add that being authentically black means that sometimes you'll stir things up. Our denomination, like other religious organizations, is a mixture of racial and ethnic groups, and because one ethnic group possesses more power than others there will always be some tension whenever those not in power challenge those who are.

RCJ: What advice or counsel do you have for those who want to be faithful to both traditions?

JD: I would admonish all black SDA preachers to be balanced in the pulpit, encouraging them to be sure to preach the Seventh-day Adventist doctrinal and prophetic themes, as well as those of liberation and the management of power. Black SDA preachers should study the lives of the prophets, since we're called to be prophetic. One thing they'll see is that the prophets were almost always misunderstood and opposed. Yet God stood by the prophets and honored them. What I want is to be able to stand before the mirror at the end of the day and see a preacher who has been thorough and balanced in preaching a uniquely Seventh-day Adventist message, as well as those disturbing biblical themes that deal with the usage and management of power.

RCJ: What are some contemporary social themes or forces impacting black SDA preaching?

JD: A significant number of black SDA pastors are obtaining graduate theological degrees, and many of them are getting their doctorates from non-SDA schools. Unfortunately, the exposure to top-rate black ministers outside the Adventist community has had somewhat of a negative impact on the church, in that some of our pastors have been smitten with the "greener grass" bug. Some of us want to be like them, perpetually comparing ourselves to these "first-day" preachers. The tendency is to discount the distinctive truths and values we have as Adventists, which is to be bemoaned. We must appreciate this wonderful message that is ours.

RCJ: How long do you nurse a sermonic idea before it matures into a sermon?

JD: Because I preach an average of two sermons a week, I have about a week to nurse a sermonic idea. Of course, many of these ideas will have been around for quite some time, but it usually takes about a week to get them ready. I know that a sermon is ready to be preached when a couple of things happen, one of which is that the sermon is in my head as a story. The Bible is really a book of stories. When I know the story I can preach it. The second thing that makes me know a sermon is ready to be preached is that I can condense the sermon into one sentence. That sentence will contain the subject, that is, what I am talking about; and the predicate or compliment, that is, what I am saying about my subject.

RCJ: Is that sentence what Haddon Robinson refers to as the "big idea?"

JD: That's absolutely right. In fact, Robinson's book, *Biblical Preaching*, has influenced my preaching more than any other book.

RCJ: You mentioned that you know a sermon is ready to be preached when you have it in your head as a story. Are you a narrative preacher then?

JD: Without a question. For me, every sermon is a narrative. There is a story behind every single text. It may be the Ten Commandments passage, but there is a story behind that passage, too. The Ten Commandments were not given in a vacuum, but to a particular people at a particular time and under particular circumstances. Paul did not theologize in a vacuum. He spoke and wrote to particular contexts, and there is a story behind all that he spoke so eloquently about. When I engage in exegesis I am not so much concerned about word studies as I am about finding the story behind the passage. If I can see the passage as a story, then I can feel it, I can act it out, I can dramatize it, I can preach it.

RCJ: Being primarily a narrative preacher, do you preach from a manuscript?

JD: I do not preach well with notes or with a manuscript. There are individuals who are able to do it, and I applaud them for being able to do so. But the more written material I have before me when I preach, the more likely I will be to bore you to death. I do not write out my sermons in manuscript form before preaching them, either. Maybe it's a lack of discipline, but I just don't do it. What I do is clarify the main idea or point of the sermon, fill up my word bank, and enter the pulpit with the idea of giving birth to the sermon. It's almost like a jazz performance in that feeling plays a big role in the outcome of the sermon. The result is that my sermons are different each time.

RCJ: As a church pastor, do you follow a sermonic calendar. If not, how do you decide what to preach from week to week?

JD: Mine is a very loose calendar. What I do is try to maintain the unique Adventist flavor of preaching while dealing with current issues at the same time. I have two services each Sabbath. The first is devoted to Adventist doctrine and prophecy and is sort of evangelistic in its focus. In the second service I deal with issues and themes on a quarterly basis. For example, during the first quarter of this year I dealt with spiritual warfare, and I dealt with relationships during the second quarter. As a church pastor I must be prophetic, priestly, and pastoral in my preaching, covering the broad themes during the year. Of course, occasions like Easter and Christmas mandate that the preacher's sermon is in sync with the season.

RCJ: How much reading do you do on average for a sermon? And what do you read and consult in preparation?

JD: Again, because of my personality, I seldom go through one book at a time. I love to read, my mother having instilled the love of reading in me at an early age. I am always reading several books simultaneously, constantly making deposits into my work bank, always looking for ways to paint work pictures. I almost always consult the *SDA Bible Commentary* for sermon material. Additionally, I use the Interpreters Bible, and I have found the Biblical Illustrator to be very helpful as far as illustrations are concerned. Of course, one must be prudent in his or her use of material from these sources if one does not want to sound like everybody else. Reading the classics is also very vital.

RCJ: What do you want your listeners to get out of the typical sermon?

JD: I'll respond by telling of an experience. Some time ago I preached at the church of a friend, Dr. Emil Peeler. I thought the message went over well. The church was boisterously excited. I took my seat without making an appeal. Peeler got up and made an appeal, and when we retired to his office at the conclusion of the service, he blasted me for preaching and not making an appeal. I got to thinking, Why do we preach? We really do preach for life change. We don't preach so that people will only understand something better, but that they know what they ought to do and be motivated to do it. For example, it is not enough that people understand forgiveness or repentance only as a concept. At the end of the day, they need to know how to repent and how to forgive and be forgiven.

RCJ: How do you bounce back from a bad sermon?

JD: Because preachers are flawed vessels, we do have bad days. God has chosen to communicate His truth through human vessels, and there are days when, for various reasons, the vessel is not as sharp. And the problem may not be spiritual, but physical and/or emotional. I deal with a bad outing by disconnecting from the preaching moment as quickly as possible. I try not to rehash or replay a bad sermon, and, incidentally, that is something I do even with a sermon that goes over well so that arrogance does not set in. I do not want a bad sermon to rob me of the confidence I need to stand up and boldly proclaim the truth of God the next time around, nor do I want arrogance to derail my next attempt. So, either way, I disconnect. By the way, this is what makes preaching tough. It is a job that is never done. When you are finished with a sermon, that sermon is definitely done. You must now focus on the next one.

RCJ: Do you listen to tapes of yourself with a view to improving your preaching?

JD: I won't recommend this to anyone, but I almost never listen to either audio or video tapes of myself, the reason being I do not want to live in the past. God has given me the ability to know my mistakes without having to listen to tapes or watch videos to discover them. Recently, I listened to a sermon I preached two years ago and the experience reminded me of the reason I don't listen to my tapes.

RCJ: Is there any other strategy you employ to prevent your confidence from lapsing into arrogance or cockiness?

JD: Preachers are like trained animals who revel in the accolades of their hearers. And the people have a catalog of nice things to say to us as they pass through the line, including, "Great sermon," and "That one was for me." We must receive those kinds of comments from our hearers with a grain of salt, so to speak. In addition, I have found it helpful to have a mentor or close friend who will tell it to us like it is. We need to hear the naked truth about our preaching from someone whose opinion we respect, if not cherish. Of course, in many cases the Lord has blessed us with wives who will tell us the honest truth.

RCJ: Talking about mentors, who were your mentors, and are you currently mentoring someone?

JD: I have a lot of friends in ministry whom I respect greatly. Dr. Benjamin Reaves continues to be one of my mentors. He is the person who taught me homiletics and who still gives me counsel and advice whenever I ask for it. Barry Black shares information about what he is reading with me, in addition to giving me pointers on effective preaching. Other colleagues with whom I trade information about preaching include Dr. Ron Smith, Dr. Emil Peeler, and Dr. Sam Hutchings, as well as my partners in the Religion Department here at Oakwood College. My father is my main mentor, though. He is the one who answers my every question with the naked truth. My brother, Jackson Doggette, and my uncle, M. M. Young, are confidants. So, too, is Dr. Mervyn Warren. I have been blessed to mentor a number of the young men who come through Oakwood year after year. Their questions and thirst for knowledge give me the opportunity to remain sharp and focused.

RCJ: How do you preach when you're under pressure or don't feel like preaching?

JD: Actually, I am motivated to preach when I'm in the midst of a storm because I'm convinced that that is when the Lord reveals Himself more. Some of my best sermons were preached when I did not feel like preaching because of some negative experience through which I was passing. During those times I truly learned what it means to depend on the Lord. So, depending on the Lord for strength is the first thing I do. Secondarily, I try to remember that I am a professional and that whether I feel like it or not, I have a job to do. Like a carpenter who may not feel like going to work but still does, I put on my work clothes, strap on my tool belt, and get to work. God always honors the sincere effort.

RCJ: What are some of the spiritual exercises you practice in preparing yourself for the preaching moment?

JD: I think it is extremely important that the preacher wait before the Lord to hear from Him before he or she mounts the pulpit. The book *Celebration of Discipline* helped me understand what meditation is all about. Waiting quietly before the Lord does not mean just sitting there expecting voices to come into your head. That can be quite dangerous. For me, the only safe way to meditate is to meditate on Scripture. That is what I do.

RCJ: How would you assess your preaching? Why are you effective in the pulpit?

JD: Others will have to answer these questions. I think, though, that I have the ability to know what it is I am trying to communicate, and I think I have a good reservoir of words on which to draw to communicate. Purpose in the sermon is key; it is vitally important. I think that people can sense, and this has to do with ethos, that I am being real when I preach. I do not take on another character or personality when I preach, having learned that I must preach in my own armor if I am going to be effective. I do not fake tears, I do not fake being hurt. If you see me crying in the pulpit, it's because I have been genuinely moved to tears. If there is any inconsistency between what the preacher is saying or doing in the pulpit and his or her life outside of the pulpit, people will know it sooner or later. And nothing destroys the effectiveness of the preacher more than a feeling on the part of his or her audience that the preacher is not for real. Let me just add that more than anything, I want to be remembered as a preacher who was sincere and relevant.

RCJ: What will your preaching be like ten or twenty years from now?

JD: Life is dynamic, society is dynamic, and personality is dynamic. As such, preaching will change. When I started preaching, I did not use drama or props as I do now. I had to change to remain relevant. I think we'll see more and more use of technology in preaching in the years ahead. Technology is not necessarily bad; yet we must not depend on technology to make us effective. In terms of content, I would hope that ten to twenty years from now I am still preaching the distinctive truths of the Adventist church. To be sure, I want to remain a black preacher, but I do not want to be responsible for letting a generation pass underneath my care without an adequate understanding of themes like the Sabbath. And our young people must hear these things from balanced preachers who know that freedom in Christ does not mean that these uniquely Adventist themes do not apply anymore.

RCJ: What advice do you have for up-and-coming preachers?

JD: I'd tell them that the development of the mind requires reading. I'd admonish them not to get their preaching information by way of videos and tapes only. I'd encourage them not to get drunk on technology. I would ask them to cultivate the art of reading, pointing out that their reading should be broad as well as deep. They must read the classics, but they must read current literature as the newspapers and magazines as well. Preachers must engage life, too, frequenting places like ball parks and barber shops where they will have the opportunity to experience life in its every day flow. As they do, they'll be able to scratch where their listeners are itching in terms of their sermon content. The preacher who is divorced from the people in society will never be an effective communicator. I seriously doubt that a sermon for young people will reach them if the preacher is unaware of their language, ways, dress, etc.

The Sermon

"Seven Steps to the Will of God"

"Just then his disciples returned and were surprised to find him talking with a woman. But no one asked, 'What do you want?' or 'Why are you talking with her?' Then, leaving her water jar, the woman went back to the town and said to the people, 'Come, see a man who told me everything I ever did. Could this be the Christ?' They came out of the town and made their way toward him. Meanwhile his disciples urged him, 'Rabbi, eat something.' But he said to them, 'I have food to eat that you know nothing about.' Then his disciples said to each other, 'Could someone have brought him food?' 'My food,' said Jesus, 'is to do the will of him who sent me and to finish his work'" (John 4:27-34).

You know the story quite well. Jesus was on His way to Galilee and had to pass through Samaria to get there. Tired and famished, He sat down at Jacob's Well to refresh Himself while His disciples went into a nearby village to procure food. Yet while they were getting their groceries, Jesus handled some other important business, that of quenching the insatiable thirst of a woman with a soiled, sordid past. He fed her hunger for meaning and purpose in life.

The disciples returned from the town carrying baskets of food, ready to give Jesus what the Master needed to be fueled up and powered up and pepped up for the trip to Galilee. But Jesus didn't have that tired, rundown look in His eyes any longer. There was a sparkle in His eyes, and there was color in His cheeks, and He looked like He had just taken a nap. Pressed to share what had happened, Jesus answered that His food was to fulfil the will of God the Father in the earth.

How do you discover the will of God for your life? While some refuse to do God's will, many others say, "Preacher, I can't figure out what God wants for me. I'm adrift on the waters of uncertainty. My life lacks focus. Every now and then I think I've figured it our, only to travel a few miles down the road and find out that I'm lost because I made a wrong turn. Oh, if I can only learn God's will for me. Help me please!"

Do you really want to find out God's will for your life? Well, I have seven steps to share with you on the subject. Follow these seven steps and you'll be on your way towards a successful life. I guarantee it. But before we get too far, you need to agree not to pull out this list of steps only when you want some big answer from God. You need to bring the little issues to God as well, because sometimes it is the little decision that leads to big failure. See, it's a matter of successive steps that determine the ultimate destination. Wise folks have learned to practice the presence of God, to pray without ceasing, and to seek God's will in all matters of life, preferring God's direction and not just God's deliverance.

STEP 1: PRE-DECIDE TO OBEY GOD. This means that before you find out what God wants, you have a made-up mind to obey. It is purposing in your heart that, no matter what God says, you will obey. I would suggest to you that some folks can't hear God's voice because they have not yet decided they will obey it. Some folks don't even want to know God's will because they're afraid God is going to want them to do something they don't want to do. You need to know that God does not have to satisfy your curious inquisitions if you do not mean business. God has promised to shine light on the path of the person who will walk in the light. In John 7:17 we read, "If any man will **do** His will, he shall **know** of the doctrine." It is true that if we decide to do, we have divine assurance that we will know.

Step One presupposes that God is smarter than we are, and requires a mental decision to follow wherever God may lead. It calls upon the sincere believer to declare, "Whatever God commands, I will do!"

STEP 2: BATHE THE ENTIRE PROCESS IN PRAYER. Why is this step so important? It is crucial because when you're seeking answers to life's questions, a cacophony of voices shout answers that don't come from God. You do know, don't you, that when you pray you're exercising the power of choice and saying, "God, control the circumstances. Silence the voices that don't speak for you so that I may discern what is right." If you fail to do that, the airways will be cluttered with dissonant voices that will frighten and confuse you. Yet, when you pray, you release God.

The prayer I usually pray goes something like this. "Lord, take complete control of this process." If I didn't exercise the power of choice in this way the devil could stand in the face of God and the unfallen worlds and declare that he didn't get a chance to make his pitch to me. Ahh, but when I release the power of God through the agency of prayer, God can respond that I chose Him, not the devil. By the way, that's why we should pray for things God already knows we need. When we exercise the power of choice, God is freed to work in our behalf. And God has a ready response for the accuser, who ever wants to declare, "It's not fair." So bathe the entire process in prayer. James 1:5 says, "If any of you lack wisdom, let him ask of God, that giveth to all men liberally, and upbraideth not; and it shall be given him." If you need to know, God will tell you. But you must ask.

STEP 3: FILTER YOUR CHOICES THROUGH THE WORD OF GOD. Psalm 110:105 declares, "Thy word is a lamp unto my feet and a light unto my path." God's word will set us in the right direction. Sometimes sincere seekers will come up with wrong conclusions and make dangerous choices thinking God is telling them to do what is in direct opposition to what God said long ago in God's Word. God is not confused, neither is God forgetful. What God has already told us through those holy men of God who wrote the Scriptures under the inspiration of the Holy Ghost hasn't slipped God's mind. God is not going to tell you to do now what He told you not to do then through His Word. If your prayer is "Lord, should I marry this man?" and the man is not a born-again Christian, God's answer will be the same. If you're praying "Lord, shall I take this job?" and the job requires that you work on God's holy day, the Sabbath, God's answer will be the same. God's will always lines up with what is contained in God's Word, and everything God declares to you must and will be clearly articulated in God's Word.

Once, a single member came to me in confidence and boldly declared, "Pastor, I know God wants me to be with Brother P." I was almost persuaded by her passionate testimony until I remembered that Brother P was married. When I informed the sister of Brother P's status, she said, "But he's so nice. I know he's my soul mate." Brother P may have been a wonderful human being, but he was the husband of another woman, and this needy single woman should have been rejoicing with the other woman for being so blessed.

If the answer to your prayer is outside of biblical parameters, then it's not for you. God's will cannot be for you to work as a bartender, spend tithe money, marry a non-believer, or seek revenge on your enemies. God sets the limits of what is and isn't acceptable. The Bible is a filter that limits the options of the faithful. It is a lamp and a light.

Before I share step number four, let me issue a warning. Use all seven steps, not just one or two. Make sure all the signs point in the same direction. You see, step number four is so subjective that without the regulating influence of the other six steps you'll be in danger of missing the mark. Step four also works best when one is converted and on speaking terms with God.

STEP 4: LISTEN FOR THE VOICE OF THE HOLY SPIRIT. "And thine ears shall hear a word behind thee saying, this is the way, walk ye in it" (Isaiah 30:21). The Holy Ghost still gives divine impressions as He did in Bible days, and those who live a devotional life and engage in daily conversations with God hear the Holy Ghost best. If you want to become familiar with the voice of the third Person of the Godhead, hang around the Bible. The Holy Ghost just loves to hover over the book He wrote. He is very impressed with His literary masterpiece and flattered by those who read it. In my mind's eye, I can see the Holy Spirit standing behind the Bible-reader saying, "Yea, when I wrote that what I really meant was. . . ." It is unwise, therefore, to try to discern the voice of the Holy Spirit from a subjective experience that is divorced from the Word. If you want to communicate with the Holy Ghost and get to know His voice, pull out His book. Read the Bible, asking the Holy Spirit questions as you do so. The Holy Ghost will be more than happy to explain Himself to you. In the process, you'll become familiar with the voice of the Holy Ghost.

Do you know that a married man can detect the sweet voice of his wife even in a noisy crowd? I can. In the midst of a riot of sounds, I am still able to pick up the frequency of the one I love—especially when La-Shunn calls my name! Let me suggest to you that although life is cluttered with busyness and noise that compete for our attention, that if we are in an intimate relationship with God we will be able to hear the still, small voice of the Holy Spirit—especially when the Holy Spirit calls out our name.

What does the voice of the Holy Spirit sound like? I really cannot answer that question, though I believe that the tone of the Spirit has a lot to do with the personality of the listener. I believe the Holy Ghost whispers to people who would melt in fear if the Holy Ghost spoke loudly to them. For other boisterous souls, the Holy Ghost, I believe, hollers every now and then. So I can't tell you exactly what the voice of the Holy Ghost sounds like, but I can guarantee that if you live a devotional life, you will know the voice of the Shepherd. (See John 10:4,5).

STEP 5: ACKNOWLEDGE PERSONAL DESIRES. Some people believe that God is so mean and cruel He gets special joy in requiring of us things we find intensely and particularly unpleasant. These folk believe that God only calls us to do things we hate doing. That is the reason some folk do not seek to know the will of God at all. They see God as a Cosmic Scrooge who wants to rain on their parade and ruin their joy. They moan, "I know God is gonna make me do the one thing in life I hate doing, so I'm not gonna ask Him. He'll make me give away all my stuff, stay single, and move to some poor country." Yet look at the contrary picture of God painted in Psalm 37:4: "Delight thyself also in the Lord; and He shall give thee the desire of thine heart."

Flip this text over and examine it from every angle. Dissect and pull out the guts of this passage and you will understand that not all of our desires are evil. It further indicates that God is happy to gift wrap and deliver some of our desires to us when we ask. Often, God sets us in a direction that is in harmony with our personal desires. God places within us aptitudes and likings, and He does it for a reason. If you like to talk, God may be calling you to a career that will let you yap. So acknowledge your personal desires and explore the possibilities they indicate. Can these desires be evil? Absolutely! That is why they must be explored and submitted to God. But you need to know that God will sometimes place desires within us to start us in the right direction.

I had to do something in life that allowed me to talk and lead. I am primarily a sanguine and secondarily a choleric. On the personality spectrum, that is the far end, indicating leadership and a bent to be extroverted. If day after day I had to do something that required I be quiet and just listen, I would blow a fuse! So God laid His hand on me and led me to a career and calling that allows me to teach, lead a church, and stand up here and yell! Thank you, Jesus. Acknowledge your likes and dislikes. Do not assume that God is going to require you to do something you hate. That's a perverted view of God. To the contrary, if you think she's ugly, God may not be leading you to ask for her hand in marriage.

STEP 6: CONSULT SPIRITUAL AND MATURE COUNSELORS. Let me start by stating unequivocally and emphatically that you cannot trust the counsel of anybody who isn't both mature and spiritual. There are some things experience alone can teach, and wisdom is a spiritual endowment that comes straight from God. If there are novices who don't know the Lord—even if they have a Ph.D. in counseling—don't consult them! They may lead you astray. They'll mess you up.

Proverbs 11:14 states, "Where no counsel is, the people fail; but in the multitude of counselors there is safety." But we must be careful with this step. We must make sure that we do not live our life based strictly on what Brother or Sister So-N-So tells us. Don't be anyone's puppet! The text clearly states that in the **MULTITUDE** of counselors there is safety.

When faced with a tough, major decision in life, you should seek out several spiritual, mature counselors for their views. What you need to look for is a general theme that rises out of their counsel. Did you get that? Look for a general theme that keeps popping up—that golden thread that is interwoven in the counsel of those who are Godly and mature. Look for and respect that golden thread. If they **ALL** tell you, "Child, I don't think it would be wise for you to marry him," don't brush it off. Instead, **RUN!**. At the very least, pay close attention.

Ellen White has a lot to say about the wisdom of Godly parents being respected. This is never more important than when a son or daughter is courting and considering marriage. In this community there are far too many stories of relationships that parents opposed being romanticized and supported. We have too many folks encouraging young couples to sneak around to avoid the "unfair scrutiny" of their "witch of a mother" and "warlord of a father", saying parents just don't understand. This pathetic practice has got to stop. The inspired pen makes it clear that godly parents are positioned by the Almighty to be the primary counselors of their children. Parents have been where their children now are and can prevent them from undue pain, heartbreak, and untold mistakes if their children will just listen. So find the golden thread and respect it.

STEP 7: SEEK GOD'S PEACE. Step number seven has come to mean a lot to me. "And let the peace of God rule in your hearts" (Col. 3:15). This word *rule* literally means *arbitrate*. This text is saying, in other words, "Let God's peace be the umpire in your soul that determines whether it is a ball or strike, fair or foul, safe or out." Let God's peace speak to you. If you've made a decision and you've started taking steps in that direction and God's peace is absent, then step on the brakes, shift into reverse, and seek the place of peace. When you make a right decision, God seals it with His peace.

After I graduated from high school I really went through some changes trying to find my niche in life. Not long after I arrived at Oakwood College I decided I was going to be an eye doctor. And that was after I had turned from my decision to be a Forest Ranger. I had decided that I was going to hang out around the water like the guy who owned Flipper and flew over the lake in an air boat every day, or hang out in the woods like the owner of Gentle Ben. Man, what a life! I was going to do that, but after I was laughed to scorn by my sisters, I decided to be an eye doctor. So I went over to the Science Department and enrolled in classes there. I did pretty well and probably would have succeeded in becoming an eye doctor. Yet I lacked peace. I was unhappy, even though I was doing OK academically. Can I explain it? No. I just know I didn't have any peace. I was antsy. I didn't feel right. When I finally got up and went over to where I belonged—the Religion and Theology Department—it was like I had found home. Did I have an easy time in the Religion and Theology Department? No! No! No! Just ask the Greek teacher who flunked me. I had some tough days in the Religion and Theology Department, Lord knows I did, but what I experienced when I got in line with God's will and ended up where I belonged was God's peace. It was like a breath of fresh air! It was like finding home! It was like the umpire had said, "Safe!"

When you are in alignment with God's perfect will, what you experience will supercede what others surmise about your situation. From the perspective of others it might look like you are utterly failing, but you'll know that you are in the right place doing the right thing, all because you're experiencing the peace of God. And this peace will settle your soul even when the strong winds are blowing. This peace will help you to stay the course even when others are telling you to turn around and go back. This peace is beyond all understanding and is more precious than fine gold.

It was this peace that steadied the gait of the Master and anchored His soul as he climbed the lonely hill to Mt. Calvary. While the crowd expected Him to tremble with fear and cry out in terror, Jesus was at peace. His calm demeanor was a silent and eloquent witness to the fact. As Jesus reached the top of the hill the crowd expected to see Him struggle to escape, but Jesus reached out for His cross even as a king reaches out for his scepter, and He wore His crown of thorns like a royal diadem. And when they nailed Him to the cross, He did not scream. And when they thrust the cruel cross into the earth, He did not cry out. He looked more like a king on an upright throne than like a criminal on a cross. This crucifixion looked more like a coronation than a crucifixion! And the event historically associated with tortured chaos was marked that day by placid dignity, all because the night before in the solitude of the Garden of Gethsemane Jesus had cried out in prayer to His Father, "Not my will, but thine be done." And He experienced what all who follow Him have come to know: WHEN YOU FIND GOD'S WILL, YOU EXPERIENCE GOD'S PEACE."

SIX

John Nixon

John Nixon is the senior pastor of the venerable Oakwood College Church of Seventh-day Adventists. He also teaches in the Department of Religion and Theology at Oakwood College, and is an associate secretary of the Ministerial Association of the North American Division of Seventh-day Adventists. Nixon is a rare breed of scholar and professional who is powerful and persuasive in the pulpit. He is a caring, compassionate pastor whose writing and preaching are enriched by intellectual discipline, pastoral experience, ethical conviction, and Holy Ghost anointing. His messages are deep and probing, and reflective of an incisive mind that engages in cutting-edge exegesis. Indeed, Nixon succeeds where others fail because of his disciplined, methodical way of unpacking Scripture. "Home at Last," the sermon that follows Nixon's interview, was delivered at the 2000 General Conference Session. It was first printed in the July 11, 2000 issue of the *Adventist Review*, and is reprinted here, with some additions, with the permission of the author.

The Interview

RCJ: When did you know for sure that God had called you to preach? And how did God call you?

JN: My experience is different from some others I've heard about. I grew up hearing stories of great preachers who, as children, would dream about becoming preachers. It wasn't until I was about 19 that the thought entered my mind, and even then the conviction was gradual. I was in college studying psychology when I felt compelled in that direction, but wasn't really sure until around graduation. One thing I remember distinctly, though, and that is the conviction came to me around the age of 19. Yet it took me years of praying and searching to become convinced that this was God's plans for me and not just my own thoughts and inclinations.

RCJ: You did not have a "burning bush" experience then. You were not hit by a bolt of lightning.

JN: No, I did not have a dream or vision. My experience was different; it was a gradual consciousness.

RCJ: Do you remember what you first preaching experience was like?

JN: I do not recall the sermon, but I know it happened when I served as a youth elder at my church in Brooklyn, New York. I remember being nervous and feeling inadequate. I also remember the congregation's response, which was very encouraging. It appears that the sermon was worth the congregation's time, and that was a sort of confirmation for me that God was calling me to preach.

RCJ: Are you saying that confirmation of your calling came through "the saints?"

JN: Though it wasn't a final confirmation, it was certainly a step in that direction. To have people who saw you grow up, who knew your all your life, and who were knowledgeable of all your misdeeds in church and school, to have those people say that they were blessed by your preaching was a strong confirmation.

RCJ: Did you have a favorite preacher back then, someone to whom you looked up?

JN: I did not really have a personal mentor, per se. There was someone whom I admired immensely and whom I tried to emulate. That person was Charles D. Brooks. There were two things that impressed me about Elder Brooks. The first thing about the preaching of Brooks that captured me was his erudition and use of language. Brooks had this incredible ability to create pictures with words, especially when he was doing narrative preaching. Listening to Brooks was like reading a good book. The other thing I admired about Elder Brooks, and this was compelling to young people, was his conviction. C. D. Brooks was a very decisive preacher who never entered the pulpit to preach something of which he was unsure. If Brooks was uncertain about something, it was not in his sermon. He knew what he was talking about when he stood up, and that gave a certain power to his words. That was very compelling to us young people back then. Young people are always looking for certainty; they want things to be clear. The certainty of Brooks impressed me.

RCJ: How do you define preaching, what is a sermon, and what is your personal theology of preaching?

JN: I currently teach a preaching class at Oakwood, so I've had some time to reflect on these questions. I've also had time to look at other people's definitions. To be informal about it, to me preaching is taking the meaning of what is behind the text and explaining it to people. I emphasize meaning because I think the preacher's job is to be an interpreter. The preacher is not the sole interpreter, or even the first interpreter; he is the current interpreter. Before the preacher is able to explain the passage to people in the here and now, he or she must know the meaning that has been given to the text. As such, a part of the preacher's preparation is studying what others have said about the text. But the preacher's task is to interpret the text in the light of the contemporary situation, and that meaning must always be seen through Jesus Christ.

RCJ: How do you go about unpacking Scripture? And how do you prepare your sermons?

JN: I believe that professional preachers, that is those of us who preach for a living, ought to have a thought-out sermon preparation process. I do not think we should ever just "wing it" in the pulpit. Now, that process has to have room in it for the Holy Spirit to do its work. I teach my students that the preparation process should take between thirty and forty hours spread over five days.

RCJ: Thirty to forty hours? Five days?

JN: Yes. In fact, I advocate that the first of those days should be devoted completely to study and reflection. I do this early in the week. Reflection is critical because without it your sermon will lack depth. During this time of reading and reflection you listen to what the passage is saying. I read the passage several times in various translations, listening to its meaning for me. I believe preachers should submit the passage to themselves first. Once you've completed this step you start the formal process, beginning with the exegesis of the passage. Exegesis has to do with digging for the literary context, the historical context, and so on. In exegesis you are trying to get back to the original meaning. The text has two horizons; it has a meaning then and it has a meaning now. And one of the first tasks of the preacher is to discover all he or she can about the original author, the original audience, the original situations, etc.

RCJ: What do you do next?

JN: I focus on the Christocentric theology of the passage. This is the timeless meaning that transcends every culture and every era. You ask questions of the passage such as, Where is God's meaning in Jesus Christ in this text? Every text has to be interpreted in Jesus Christ or the sermon will not be a Christian sermon. This applies whether the passage is from the Old Testament or the New Testament. Once I've discovered the Christocentric theology of the passage, I relate the passage to the contemporary situation. The last thing I do is put the text into some homiletic form, which is usually suggested by the text itself.

RCJ: I take it, then, that it would be a challenge to say that you are primarily a topical, textual, narrative, or expository preacher?

JN: Yes, the reason being that that thought is not as important as the sermon preparation process itself. The form you use varies, it being totally dependent on the passage.

RCJ: Where do you look for illustrations? Recently, a student in one of my classes talked about your ability to come up with captivating stories to illustrate your sermons. Where does that gift come from?

JN: I tell my students that when I was their age, coming up with great illustrations was my plague. Yet to answer the question, I look everywhere for stories. When I was younger I bought books of illustrations, but I don't anymore. Preachers must develop what I call a "homiletic bias," where they listen, see, and read everything through a bias of preparation to preach. I use to walk around with a pad to jot stuff down on, but now I have a telephone with a voice memo that I use to record ideas for illustrations. I think everything is fair game for sermon illustrations. I need to add something that may be somewhat controversial.

RCJ: What is that?

JN: I believe that a story may be changed by the preacher and used as an illustration. Preachers are not news reporters who are bound to give an exact rendering of an incident. We use stories to illustrate what we are trying to convey theologically. Because of this, we can change a story, although we must not mislead people to believe that the story is factual.

RCJ: Some preachers take a skeleton outline with them into the pulpit. Others are manuscript preachers. Still others preach without notes. Which do you do?

JN: For the first five or six years of my ministry I was an outline preacher, but I've become a manuscript preacher.

RCJ: That's interesting. Usually it's the other way around. People usually begin as manuscript preachers, moving on to becoming outline or extemporaneous preachers. Why the reverse with you?

JN: Let me say this before moving on. I take a manuscript into the pulpit and I follow it pretty faithfully for the first quarter or so of the sermon. After that, I begin to use it as more of an outline. Even then, there are times in the sermon when I will return to a word-for-word use of the manuscript, doing so whenever I want to be accurate with facts and words. Because language is very important with me, I spend a lot of time thinking about how to couch certain things, and once I get it right I want to make sure that I say it right, too. That's one reason I carry a manuscript with me into the pulpit. I want to be as precise as possible with certain things, and this is critical in narrative preaching, which I do a lot of. Now, there is an art to using a manuscript effectively. You want to be sure not to keep your head buried in the manuscript, and you do not want to sound like you're reading a book. It takes a lot of practice to do manuscript preaching effectively.

RCJ: As a manuscript preacher, do you stay behind the pulpit for the entire sermon?

JN: No. I do move about. There are a couple of things I learned recently about speakers who move about. First, I learned that you keep people's attention more. That is why we're seeing more and more TV preachers moving about. Second, and I just read this recently, I learned that men think better when they are on their feet and moving. The brain has something to do with this, and apparently it is not the same for women. Since learning this I've started moving more when I preach. To be sure, I start out stationary, but as the sermon develops there is more movement on my part. One last thing on this point, I almost always leave the pulpit area now and go into the congregation when I make my appeals. This is something I did not do before.

RCJ: Do you rehearse your sermons?

JN: My brother does that; I've never done it. Back in college, guys would go to the chapel to practice their preaching, and I would hear them from my dorm room. I was never able to get into that. Now, I do preach my sermons in my head, always hearing them in my head before putting them to paper. But the talking out loud thing I do not do. It works for other people, but not for me.

RCJ: As a manuscript preacher who gives much thought to what he wants to say and writes it down exactly how he wants it said, how do you go about letting the Holy Spirit have His way with you in the pulpit?

JN: I believe the Holy Spirit is involved in both the preparation and delivery processes. I also believe that the Holy Spirit will not reveal some things until you are in the pulpit, making sticking to your manuscript a challenge. I have had the experience of skipping over material in my manuscript and changing something therein while preaching. I have never, however, completely changed a sermon or abandoned one altogether in the pulpit. I've gone in different directions and eliminated a particular closing illustration, etc., when I've instinctively responded to the moment and the Holy Spirit's leading. You see, when we prepare to preach it is just not about preparing the sermon but also about preparing ourselves. Preaching is a spiritual enterprise that is bound to fail if the Holy Spirit is not involved.

RCJ: Even when you are prepared to the hilt, sometimes you just don't "hit it." How do you bounce back from a sermon that "missed?"

JN: I teach my students that if they preach a biblical sermon that is thoroughly prepared, they will not waste people's time. If the foundation of the sermon is the substance of Scripture as interpreted in Jesus Christ, the sermon will not miss the mark. Even if the sermon does not go over as you expect it to and the audience does not respond as you think it should, a sermon grounded in the Word of God is never a waste of people's time. The preacher can be confident in the knowledge that he or she gave the congregation something to chew on.

RCJ: That you are the senior minister of the Oakwood College Church speaks to the fact that you are considered an outstanding preacher. How have you been able to remain humble?

JN: Part of the weekly preparation process is removing yourself out of the way and concentrating on being used to God's glory. As a preacher I should only aspire to be used by God. And so every time I preach I have the task of removing myself. I tell young preachers that if they are too confident or too nervous they have not succeeded in removing themselves from the picture. Overconfidence means you are thinking too much of yourself and your charisma, and a complete lack of confidence means that you have not put your confidence in God. Preachers have to move beyond listening to the reviews people have of their preaching. Jesus was beyond that, according to John 2:25. Even when the people praised Him, Jesus knew that that was the human element at work in them. And He knew that they would be cursing him soon. So preachers have to preach and live based on the opinion of God, not people.

RCJ: Let's switch gears for a moment and talk about black preaching. What is black preaching, and what distinguishes it form other kinds of preaching?

JN: I think there is an element in black preaching that has to do with form, though that is not the element on which we should place the most emphasis. There are those who speak of the black style, going so far as to say that some preachers of a different racial or ethnic group have a "black style" of preaching. Supposedly, the black style is lively and interactive. I believe there is some truth to this. I also believe that the delivery style of the preacher should be adaptable, and I don't think a preacher should force his or her style on an audience.

RCJ: What do you mean by that? Please unpack that for me.

JN: I've pastored in different settings and different cities, and to different age and ethnic groups. To be heard and understood, I've had to adapt my style. There is an incident that stands out in my mind that aptly illustrates what I am talking about. I've discovered that white males are the individuals least likely to tell you anything about your sermon when you are through. Blacks, perhaps not surprisingly, are the ones who most often tell you about your sermon. White males just do not. They just leave without saying anything. On this particular occasion some white men came to me and told me that they had been moved by my sermon, and that the thing that moved them was my "low-key" preaching. They said that the power of my sermon was in the message, not in the "force" of my preaching. Apparently, the fact that I had not raised my voice, something they said would have interfered with the message, impressed them. This is one reason I do not put much stock in the form aspect of preaching. I believe that a black preacher, like any other preacher, must be adaptable.

RCJ: What about the content of black preaching?

JN: Yes, I can say much about the content of black preaching. I think that the content of black preaching came into existence as a response to the direction the Christian church in the West had taken as it relates to certain themes of the gospel. Black preaching took us back to themes such as God's special care for the downtrodden and the oppressed, themes that are unmistakable in the Old and New Testaments. When God talks about how He judges a nation, when God talks about how He judges kings and rulers, when God talks about how He judges His own people, God inevitably is raising key themes of Scripture that black preaching takes rather seriously.

RCJ: Black preaching and Adventist preaching. Are they mutually exclusive?

JN: I agree with those who say they are mutually exclusive, hastening to elaborate that they are mutually exclusive to the extent that they are practiced badly. I think when black preaching and Adventist preaching are done properly and appropriately they are compatible, not incompatible. That is to say that black preaching is biblical, not just political. The content of black preaching can become nothing but politics if it focuses on the oppressed alone. It can be concerned only with bringing power to me. When black preaching does that it has left truth behind. When Adventist preaching becomes apologetic, it too has left truth behind. So I think when black preaching remains biblical, and when Adventist preaching remains Christ-centered, they are at heart complimentary.

RCJ: You have been preaching now for over a quarter of a century? How has preaching changed in that time?

JN: I hope Adventist preaching is coming back to being more Christ-centered and more gospel-oriented instead of just being doctrine-oriented.

We had a lively class discussion about this recently at Oakwood. A student wanted to know how you go about preaching the gospel in a culture that is basically Christian. How do you preach Jesus and the cross to people who already know about them? What people don't know about is the Sabbath, the sanctuary, and things like that. These are questions for Adventist preachers, and the questions themselves are a revelation that we have veered off the path. You see, if you are preaching the Sabbath, the Ten Commandments, and the Sanctuary outside of the context of the gospel, your doctrinal preaching is distorted. How can you preach doctrine without the gospel? What is the meaning of doctrine apart from the gospel? It's not a question of whether people understand the gospel or not; it's a question of explaining the gospel to them in a way that includes these distinctively Adventist understandings of Scripture. We explain them not apart from the gospel, but in the context of the gospel. Our job as Adventist preachers is to center Adventist beliefs in Jesus Christ so that we are not just defining our belief system but presenting Christ.

RCJ: Why do you think people consider you an outstanding preacher?

JN: I don't think I know how to answer that question. I can answer, however, how I would like to be remembered as a preacher. I'd like to be remembered as somebody who taught the gospel. The biggest compliment I ever received came from a woman who said to me, "I want to know when you'll be preaching next because I have a dear friend I want to bring to church. I know that if I bring my friend when you are in the pulpit my friend is going to hear about Jesus Christ."

RCJ: If you had one last sermon to preach, what would it be?

JN: The most meaningful and powerful thing we can ever say in the pulpit is what I once heard T. Marshall Kelly talk about. He said that the real meaning of salvation is inward, not outward. Something has to happen in your heart and nature that even you cannot explain. It is something that with all your education, prowess, discipline and accomplishments you cannot accomplish. This inward change takes place only as you come under the control of the Holy Spirit. Once the change takes place, you preach about it, like Jesus did. Jesus preached Himself, and our task is to preach what He preached.

RCJ: One last question. What counsel, what advice, would you like to share with young preachers?

JN: There are two answers to that question; one is practical, the other is personal. On the practical side, I would tell them to become deeply spiritual persons who practice the spiritual disciplines. Prayer, Bible study, meditation, and service are things that should be an integral part of the life of every preacher. I would also encourage every young preacher to find someone to whom they become accountable. The person may be their spouse, a fellow pastor, or a dear friend. Whomever, it must be someone who has the permission to criticize every area of their life, including their ideas. Preachers must stay on the spiritual track.

RCJ: What about the personal side?

JN: On the personal level, I would counsel someone just starting out in the preaching ministry to avoid all forms of pride and self-reliance. Validating yourself or your preaching by what others have to say should be shunned. The Word of the Lord is not a Word in search of acceptance; it is a word in search of submission and obedience. The first priority of a preacher is not to preach a word that people like, but to preach a word people need. And what we need is often not readily apparent to us, a fact Scripture makes plain. So the preacher must preach a word in search of submission and in search of obedience, and he or she can do this to the extent that he or she has submitted to the word. That is the counsel I would like to share with young preachers as they seek to develop their technical skills.

The Sermon

"Home at Last"

"And he said unto them, It is not for you to know the times or the seasons, which the father hath put in his own power. But ye shall receive power, after that the Holy Ghost is come upon you; and ye shall be witnesses unto me both in Jerusalem, and in all Judaea, and in Samaria, and unto the uttermost parts of the earth. And when he hath spoken these words, while they beheld, he was taken up; and a cloud received him out of their sight. And while they looked stedfastly toward heaven as he went up, behold, two men stood by them in white apparel; which also said, Ye men of Galilee, why stand ye gazing up into heaven? This same Jesus, which is taken up from you into heaven, shall so come in like manner as ye have seen him go into heaven" (Acts 1:7-11).

It is the dawn of a new age for the followers of Christ, the transition into a new dispensation. Just completed, in the heroic life and ministry of Jesus of Nazareth, is the age of the Messiah. The Son of God has come and lived and died in exact accordance with Bible prophecy, doing only that which was appointed to Him by the Father.

The Star out of Jacob has fed His flock like a Shepherd, carrying the young lambs in His bosom. He has spent His life binding up the brokenhearted, proclaiming liberty to the captives, and opening the prisons of the bound. He has loosed the bonds of wickedness and undone the heavy burdens of the oppressed. Faithful to His calling all the way to Calvary, He was wounded for our transgressions and bruised for our iniquities, the chastisement of our peace was upon Him, and with His stripes we are healed. The first Advent has been a smashing success (Num. 24:17; Isa. 40:11; 61:1; 53:5)!

Jesus has accomplished His mission to save the world, and now, with His companions looking on, He returns to the Father who sent Him. He has already spoken His last words with their hearts pounding so loud you can hear them, and now as He raises His hand in final blessing, Jesus slowly mounts the air. They did not see Him rise from the tomb, but the disciples behold Him now, and an awesome silence prevails as they stretch their necks and stand on their toes, straining to embrace Him to the very last.

The One who changed their lives forever is taken from them in the providence of God. But in His departure a dual promise is given upon which their hopes can stand. It is not a promise for the eleven only, but for all believers in every generation. It is a dual promise: it is the promise of the Holy Spirit and the promise of the second coming of Christ. Jesus is not gone forever; His spirit abides with us here and now. Jesus is not gone forever; He will come again in power and great glory. Jesus is coming again!

How thrilling it must have been to be a Christian in the first century, to live in the age of the apostles. What an honor to know the original twelve, to hear their sermons, read their letters, witness their miracles, and to have beating in your breast the fervent hope of the soon return of the Lord. All Christians were Adventists in the original church. The hope of the Second Coming was the fire that ignited every soul!

There was no dispute, in the beginning, over whether the coming would be literal or figurative. There was no dispensationalist controversy, and no debate over how the world would end, whether by some cosmic catastrophe or some nuclear accident. Still alive in the original church were those who had heard the teachings of Jesus from His own lips, who had eaten miracle bread from His own hands, who had had their eyes opened and their ears unstopped by word of His power, who had seen demons tremble and run for cover at the sound of His name!

Still testifying from town to town were those who had heard firsthand heaven's promise: "He will come as you have seen Him go."

Notice the careful precision of language in the angel's announcement. It is specific in an intentional way. The two men dressed in white refer to the manner of Christ's return by noting the manner of His departure. Here is why it is important that the disciples saw Him go; the second Advent is based on the ascension.

If His going was *to* heaven, then His coming back will be *from* heaven:

"For the Lord himself shall descend from heaven with a shout, with the voice of the archangel, and with the trump of God; and the dead in Christ shall rise first" (1 Thess. 4:16).

If He was caught up in the clouds, then He must return in the clouds: "Wherefore if they shall say unto you, Behold, he is in the desert; go not forth; behold, he is in the secret chambers; believe it not (Matt. 24:26).

If all the disciples saw Him leave, then every eye will see Him return: "For as the lighting cometh out of the east, and shineth even unto the west; so shall also the coming of the Son of man be" (verse 27).

It will be just as He said. It is the word of God that is at stake, and He cannot lie; Jesus is coming again!

Here is the teaching we have faithfully preached for more than 150 years, the Millerite disappointment notwithstanding. This aspect of the promise has been our occupation and the meaning of our name, Seventh-day Adventist—but it is not all the angels had to say. Together with the statement on the manner of Christ's coming is a statement of identity. The angels said "this same Jesus," and there is meaning in these words as well.

The Same Jesus

All of our focus has been on the event of the Parousia itself and on its ominous signs. But false Christs and false prophets are not the only dangers of the last days. There is another danger more threatening to the people of God, something worse than beasts and dragons, though we have not watched for it as carefully. When we recall the First Advent we are reminded that the Jewish priests and leaders–the keepers of the oracles of God–did not welcome the newborn King. They knew the prophecy of the First Advent so well that they could explain it to Herod, but they did not go to visit the new King. Bethlehem was only six miles away!

Since it was known that the Messiah would come through Jewish bloodlines, why was there not a great celebration in Jerusalem? "The advent of Christ was the greatest event which had taken place since the creation of the world. The birth of Christ, which gave joy to the angels of Heaven, was not welcome to the kingly powers of the world. Suspicion and envy were aroused in king Herod, and his wicked heart was planning his dark purposes for the future. The Jews manifested a stupid indifference to the story of the wise men" (Ellen G. White, in *Review and Herald*, Dec. 24, 1872). This was the reception Jesus got the first time around, and it was not just from priests and leaders.

We sing about the shepherds in the field who heard the angel's song, but do we realize that most of Israel did not acknowledge Christ's coming at all? "He came unto his own, and his own received him not" (John 1:11). The first coming of Jesus was a public relations disaster, a huge nonevent. His childhood and youth were passed in obscurity. The citizens of Nazareth had Him for thirty years and did not know their visitation. When he returned home to preach after His baptism, the people He grew up with refused to hear His message and tried to throw Him from a cliff! "He was in the world, and the world was made by him, and the world knew him not" (John 1:10).

Except to receive His gifts and blessings, most people had little to do with Jesus. And when they really understood what His kingdom was about, they stopped following Him altogether (See John 6:66). A low-class, uneducated Nazarene of suspicious parentage who socialized with prostitutes and tax collectors was not their idea of a Messiah.

And the message to us is this: the Jesus who is coming back is the same Jesus who was here before. He is today, 2000 years later, just as unconventional, just as common as He always was—He is not impressed with us. He is not coming to fulfill our dream, unless our dream is His dream.

Are we ready to meet this Jesus? It is an urgent question for the last generation of believers—we know that Jesus is coming, but do we know the Jesus who comes? He has not become Westernized since the Adventist Church was raised up in the West. He has not become middle class because we have embraced middle-class values. He has not changed His mind about how salvation happens to harmonize with our denominationalism. He is the same Jesus He always was: the same Jesus who taught that the kingdom of God belongs to children and that the only true greatness is the greatness of humility; the Jesus who crossed social barriers of every description to reach all people for the kingdom of God; the Jesus who defied corrupt church authority and called scribes and Pharisees hypocrites to their faces; the Jesus who would not break the yoke of Roman oppression, but taught His followers instead to love the oppressor and pray for their redemption; the Jesus who was unorthodox, unpredictable, uncontrollable, and unsafe.

Jesus is coming whether we know Him or not, but if we do not know Him, He is not coming for us.

And we must clarify what we mean by "know," because the Bible rejects the concept of salvation by special knowledge. This was the claim of Gnosticism. There is no esoteric, hidden knowledge by which salvation may be privately gained. Doctrinal superiority is not the key to heaven's gate. The unpublished writings of Ellen White are not the secret passageway to the kingdom of God. There are all on CD-ROM now anyway.

On the other hand, salvation by grace does involve knowledge, but what must be known, first and foremost, is not a set of facts—not even Bible facts. The knowledge that saves is personal knowledge, and the Person is Jesus. I do not agree that the emphasis on Jesus in the Adventist Church today constitutes a swing of the pendulum too far in the other direction. Jesus is not some extreme on the fringes of faith; He is the very center of all our belief and practice. We can never emphasize too much the need for maintaining an intimate relationship with Jesus. He is everything to us.

I read of a boy living by the sea who loved nothing more than building castles in the sand. Every day after school he would build them of different shapes and sizes, and every day a group of bullies from school would destroy them. Then one day, on a tip from his grandpa, the boy put chunks of concrete and cinder block in the base of the castles. The next time the bullies came to destroy, they stubbed their toes and feet.

Even castles made of sand become impregnable when they are built upon a rock. Believers are vulnerable too—to the attacks of the enemy, to the weaknesses of the flesh. But when their lives are built on the rock, they are strong to withstand anything. This rock is Jesus—not facts *about* Jesus, not blessings *from* Jesus, not even just the teachings *of* Jesus, but Jesus Christ Himself.

It is not getting people to doctrine, but getting people to Jesus, that is the priority of our mission, and once they get to Him they will be shocked at what they find. Jesus is both more gracious and more terrifying than people think. He will lift them into heavenly places like no one else, and He will hurt their feelings like no one else!

In the question of Luke 18:8, "When the Son of man cometh, will he find faith on the earth?" Jesus is not asking about faith in the doctrine or faith in the denomination. Jesus is looking for faith in Himself. If we believe only what He says, we do not truly believe. We must believe in Him. Only then is Christ formed in us, and we come to have His view in everything. There are two elements to readiness—right relationship and the knowledge of where we are; that is, knowing Jesus and knowing the times. So while we are watching the signs and the beast, we better not forget to watch the cross. Being ready for Jesus to come means being ready for Jesus.

There is a double blessing in the coming of Jesus—It is not only in two stages; it is in two persons. The Jesus we await is the Jesus we already possess. And the promise of the Parousia is the hope that fuels our joy, while the "when" of the Parousia is a matter of indifference since we are ready at all times. Jesus Christ Himself is the our readiness.

The story is told of J. L. McIlhenny, maker of Louisiana hot sauce. In creating the best possible product, McIlhenny had a secret that kept him ahead of his competitors. Each year at harvest time McIlhenny personnally supervised the gathering of the peppers. He carried with him into the fields a red stick, a baton rouge. It was the perfect shade of red for peppers just right for harvest. He held his stick against the crop to determine which peppers were ready, and only the best peppers were used to make the greatest hot sauce in the world.

Jesus has a baton rouge He will carry into the harvest field of the world. It is dipped in Jesus' own blood and bears the perfect shade of red for humans ready to enter His kingdom. Only those whose lives have been stained with that blood will see God face to face.

SEVEN

Walter L. Pearson

Walter L. Pearson is a former associate secretary of the Ellen G. White Estate and associate director of Evangelism and Church Growth in the Ministerial Department of the General Conference of Seventh-day Adventists. He is currently the director/speaker of the Breath of Life Telecast and a general field secretary of NAD. Pearson has conducted successful evangelistic campaigns in the West Indies, Europe, and Africa, and is known for his sharp wit and humor, as well as his "sanctified imagination." His sermons reflect intense introspection and study, and Pearson's penchant for spinning the biblical story in creative ways that capture and hold the interest of his hearers is legendary. Pearson was the first SDA preacher to be inducted into the Martin Luther King, Jr. Board of Preachers and Scholars at Morehouse College in Atlanta, Georgia, and is in demand to speak at churches, colleges, universities, youth rallies, convocations, and camp meetings. "Called to the Dry Bones District" was delivered to students at the Seventh-day Adventist Theology Seminary at Andrews University.

The Interview

RCJ: At what age did you know you were called to preach? What led to your conviction?

WLP: My earliest recollections are difficult to date. Not unlike most children, I cherished "flavor of the month" professional inclinations based on the most recent images. I began to think seriously about my inclinations being a "call" at 13 when I preached my first sermon. Years later when I preached to a group of prisoners whom the warden had summoned abruptly from a baseball game and saw several of them indicate a desire to accept Christ as the result of my feeble effort, I experienced firsthand the thrill of having God use me. That initiated a process, but it was not until I was a student at Pine Forge Academy that I was convicted of the call to preach and positively influence people.

RCJ: Who were the preachers you admired back then? And did anyone in particular mentor you?

WLP: The pastors I admired in my childhood were D. B. Reid and Edwin Humphrey. After my decision to pursue ministry, E. E. Cleveland, Charles Bradford, Samuel Myers, and Charles D. Brooks were primary among those to whom I looked for inspiration. Harold Cleveland became my mentor, both because I admired him and because he was willing to make the time for such a task. He was my pastor during my formative teenage years, the minister whom I chose to study while at Oakwood, and the pastor under whose direction I did my internship.

RCJ: What is your understanding or theology of preaching? How do you define a sermon?

WLP: Both my culture and my philosophy put preaching at the center of ministry. I am convinced that Jesus speaks to humankind through the foolishness of preaching. I believe that faith comes by hearing the Word of God and that this hearing is most often experienced through preaching. I believe that the revelation of divine power through the spoken Word is the recurring miracle which energizes and sustains the church. After effective preaching has been done, there is an endless list of important duties which contribute to church growth and nurture. But without preaching, it is difficult to identify the called-out ones. A sermon is God communicating a divine message to humanity, through humanity, by a process which He alone makes effective.

RCJ: Where do your messages come from? In other words, how do you decide what to preach?

WLP: My reflex response would be to say from God, but they are not always directly from Him. The questions and needs of people form sermons. Events evoke sermons. Books inspire sermons. Situations require sermons. Preachers project thoughts which take root in the hearts of other preachers and mature into other sermons. At length, life experiences call for sermons. Nevertheless, God must be the One who gives the sermon, directly and indirectly. With all of these elements in mind, I seek to know what God has to say to individuals.

RCJ: What routines and resources do you use in sermon preparation? How much time is involved, on average, in the process?

WLP: I maintain a separate personal study regimen which is not intended to be a sermon resource. It cannot, however, divorce itself from that purpose. Though one does not supplant the other or intentionally parallel it, personal devotion sometimes informs preaching in a very powerful manner. Having said that, let me hasten to say that my favorite exercise is to actively listen as I let the Bible speak. It pays to let the Word lead. When I fail to understand, I consult resources and press until the meaning is clear. When one has the luxury of setting aside what is not ready–to let it simmer—the results can be fulfilling. I try and stretch my horizons by reading passages which are not naturally interesting, seeking to understand why they were written. Sometimes I read books that are dull, dense, or written in unattractive language just to stretch my mind.

RCJ: Anything else?

WLP: I am always on the lookout for illustrations, and the true, contemporary illustration is the best for me. I jot down notes to myself. I record them electronically. I listen to people who are not faithful members of the flock so that my preaching does not become inordinately affected by or directed to "the choir." When I was a church pastor, I would ride the public transit system from one end to the other, east to west, then north to south, to catch the cadence of the public discourse. I did this so that I could speak to the audience which I hoped to draw. I wanted to know the issues which were relevant in the marketplace.

RCJ: How much time do you spend in sermon preparation?

WLP: Although my preparation time varies, I have learned that the usual time required to put a good sermon together is about sixteen hours. Since the actual construction of a sermon is a solitary exercise for me, I often prepare my sermons in the middle of the night or early morning.

RCJ: Do you spend more time working on any part of the sermon, e.g., the introduction, or the appeal? Do you think any one part of a sermon is more important than another part?

WLP: The thought which represents the pivotal thrust of a sermon consumes most of my time. Since every preacher basically uses the same book as a resource, the thought which sets a familiar element in an unusual frame is generally my point of concentration. Samuel Myers once told me that a familiar room becomes new and interesting if you enter it from a different door. Another respected peer shared the concept that the preacher is not unlike a movie director because he can select the actors, the scenery, the lighting, and the costumes to make an old story seem new. The preacher can also invert the sequence or even start in the middle to press home the point. Some of these methods can add impact as long as the preacher is faithful to the message of the text. According to Ellen White, Jesus used the imagination to capture His audience. Similarly, I want to highlight a central thought which seizes the imagination without wresting Scripture. This is where I devote most of my time. The appeal is probably the most important part of the sermon even when the sermon doesn't call for an overt response like the ones traditionally associated with evangelism. Lately, my appeal is guided by the Holy Spirit in a more pronounced fashion. I give as much thought and prayer to the appeal as I used to before. However, I leave more latitude for the Spirit to direct. The Holy Spirit never fails.

RCJ: How do you know that a sermon is ready to be preached? Do you ever give a sermon a "dry run," field testing it in order to preach it more effectively again?

WLP: When I draw a line through the sermon and naturally connect every element, the sermon is ready. It is sometimes difficult to know what is enough and what is too much, what should be included and what should be eliminated. I use a modular approach because it allows me to add or drop material based on my impressions from the Lord, as well as from more mundane sources. Before I started traveling extensively, I rarely repeated sermons. Of course, one would be foolish to take a poor sermon to a guest speaking appointment. Yet the occasion sometimes calls for sermons which may not have been well received elsewhere. Now that I am in a different pulpit practically every Sabbath, and because I am always in search for the best material for broadcasting, I do "road test" sermons.

RCJ: Please elaborate on the differences between evangelistic and other kinds of preaching.

WLP: Evangelistic sermons must avoid broad assumptions concerning the piety of the audience. As annoying as it may be for believers of long standing, the evangelist has to contextualize the message in favor of the secular individual. Universal truths should season early sermons in a series. As the audience gains confidence in the preacher (both because the Lord engenders it on the preacher's behalf and because the speaker evinces a relationship with Christ by precept and example) unique biblical teachings may be treated with confidence. Evangelistic sermons are typically topical. "Line upon line and precept upon precept" is the mantra of the evangelist. Most pastors thrive on expository or narrative preaching. I have used a fusion of the narrative and the topical approach in order to keep the interest of post-modern audiences.

RCJ: You are known for your anecdotes, imagery, and humor. Where do those characteristics come from? And what have you done to cultivate them over the years?

WLP: In my admittedly biased opinion, I would have to say that my mother was the best among a family of engaging readers and story tellers. Her parents, as well as my aunts and uncles, repeated anecdotes with wit and wisdom that improved with each repetition. A teacher for practically all her life, Mom could read a story and make it so real that children would try and fix their eyes on objects in thin air. She was headed for a Howard University education with dreams to be the next Dorothy Dandridge when she and my grandmother heard the powerful preaching of J. G. Thomas under a tent in Mobile, Alabama. My father and his family were also well versed in the practical use of the persuasive arts. They could convey more with a raised eyebrow or a facial twist than most could with a thousand words. They could talk way into the night without benefit of any media accompaniment. So, when it comes to communication, what seems contrived to some is only natural for me. I am blessed with native gifts which God has used to His glory because I dedicated them to him.

RCJ: What about your humor?

WLP: I do not write humor into my sermons. I seldom plan to use humorous anecdotes. In fact, I am sometimes surprised at the audience reaction as I preach. What I'm trying to convey is that my humor is not intentional. It is natural. Since a very providential conversation with Samuel Myers (a very humorous speaker) early in my ministry, I do not repress my humor. I try my best to allow the Lord to employ my personality to His glory. Having read many of her sermons and speeches, I have a much better grasp of what the messenger had in mind when she seemed to condemn all humor. I'm always monitoring my presentations, but I am finally free in Jesus.

RCJ: When does imagination turn into eisegesis?

WLP: When it serves itself instead of facilitating a true understanding of what God is saying through His Word. The context will often dictate how much and in what manner imagination may be employed. An understanding of the context is extremely important in this regard. What will assist one audience in grasping true meaning will hinder another.

RCJ: As a rule, do you preach with notes? How much difference do you think preaching without notes makes?

WLP: During my last ten years as a pastor, I rarely used notes. A simple explanation is that my memory seemed to improve as an answer to prayer, a prayer I probably should have prayed during my educational experience. It was a blessing for me. I was free to concentrate on the reactions of my audience and that helped me to communicate more effectively. More importantly, I began to recognize divine instructions which sometimes seemed almost audible. I have concluded that God was always directing, but I was too involved with notes before to take notice.

RCJ: How much attention do you give to wording in the sermon?

WLP: An amazing amount. In order to sound spontaneous, I often memorize phrases and even paragraphs. It is intended to come off seamlessly, and usually does when I've prepared well. Under optimum circumstances, I write the modules which serve as building blocks for the sermon using my unabridged dictionary and thesaurus. Often I go back and clean up the language because I tend to use old words. The effort is worthwhile because without it I tend to repeat words and phrases ad nauseam.

RCJ: Much ado has been made about black preaching? What's your definition and understanding of black preaching?

WLP: Lately, I think creative Afrocentric minds and obsessive Eurocentric minds have hyped the terminology up so much that it is overblown. Black preachers justifiably want to give black preaching the importance it deserves. Unintentionally, we have described it beyond reality. When the descendants of Europe want to gain intellectual mastery over an entity, they tend to quantify it, qualify it, dissect and label it, until it is essentially foreign to those who introduced it. As soon as "white preaching" is defined in that way, I will feel impelled to do the same with black preaching. We know that black preaching varies so significantly from denomination to denomination and from church to church that it can barely be housed within the same universe.

RCJ: What do you do to proclaim a distinctly Seventh-day Adventist message while remaining true to the black preaching tradition?

WLP: I see no tension at all between the Adventist message and the black preaching tradition. To be sure, there are some minor technical differences here and there, but the two are not mutually exclusive. Black preaching is audacious; it is a kind of in-your-face preaching that is broad, covering a range of subjects often neglected by others. In that sense, the black preacher is very much at home preaching Seventh-day Adventist truths, which are holistic and address the total person. Black preaching is unambiguously biblical, as is Adventist preaching. Black preachers proclaim the truth–with an attitude. When the black preacher stands in the pulpit, he or she does so saying, "I have the truth and I have a right to proclaim it." That is what the Adventist preacher does also when he or she stands in the pulpit. Now, it is true that the Adventist preacher could be a little more prophetic at times, as it relates to pointing out the injustices and inequities in society. That is where black preaching has to step up to the plate, and that should be natural because that is biblical.

RCJ: As an evangelist, you rarely preach a sermon without making an appeal. What is the secret to effective appeals?

WLP: For me, the appeal must be ethical. The preacher has access to the heart of the hearer, and that is something that the preacher should not take lightly. It is an honor and a privilege that God allows. We should not misuse that privilege by pushing people to make a decision. The preacher should refrain from using emotionalism as he or she appeals to the individual to decide for Christ. We must lay out as best as we can that for which we are asking, making sure that what the individual offers up is informed consent. Again, preachers should shun emotionalism like the plague, though it is not unethical to appeal to the emotions.

RCJ: What's the difference?

WLP: I've sold everything from encyclopedias to cars, and I know that you cannot sell anything without appealing to the emotions. A salesperson can convince a person intellectually about what he or she is selling, but that salesperson will hardly ever make a sale until he or she connects the prospect to the product emotionally. When I sold cars my strategy was to give the prospective buyer all the pertinent information about the car first. Next, I would invite the prospective buyer to take a ride in the car. Smelling the leather seats, feeling the steering wheel, and, perhaps most important, having his neighbors see him driving this new car, did more to convince the prospective buyer to buy the car than telling him every thing I knew about disc brakes and rank and pinion steering. The parallel for us, in terms of getting a person to make a decision, is to have that person experience Jesus. Once a man or a woman sees Jesus clearly and experiences Jesus's magnitude, he or she will fall in love with Him. The best and most lasting decisions are not based on fear but love—love for Jesus Christ! Convincing people about the Mark of the Beast and scaring them about the ill effects of receiving it is an unethical appeal to emotionalism. Getting them to experience and love Jesus is an ethical appeal to the emotions.

RCJ: How did you develop your style of preaching? And in which areas do you think you still need to grow?

WLP: I am my most severe critic. This may surprise people, but I've never preached a sermon with which I was pleased. Always, I leave the pulpit saying to myself, "I've got to do this better. I have to improve on that." I'm always trying to think of ways to improve. Over the years I've had some good role models, a pantheon of stars, that I've analyzed, trying to determine what they did extremely well and the reasons behind their style. My goal was not to do mimic these preachers, though initially people did say that I sounded like an admixture of Cleveland and Bradford. Four or five years into my preaching ministry, I started praying for an excellence in preaching. I did not want to be a great preacher, just an excellent exponent of truth and one adept at lifting up Jesus Christ. To stretch myself, I also preach sermons I do not normally or ordinarily do. For example, I am best at what Benjamin Reaves calls "stories told." Narrative preaching, not topical preaching, is more fun for me; narrative preaching is my gravity center. Yet, to get out of my comfort zone, to stretch myself, to grow as a preacher, I'll get out of narrative preaching from time to time. I do not want to be a one-horse preacher, so I utilize the topical genre, especially in my evangelistic preaching, ever so often.

RCJ: What counsel do you have for beginning preachers? In other words, what is the secret of great preaching?

WLP: First off, who the preacher is is infinitely more important than what the preacher says and how the preacher sounds. The preacher must first become what God wants the preacher to be. The least talented preacher who is fully dedicated to God will be more effective than the most talented preacher who lacks a personal relationship with God. Dedication is more important than talent; it will supercede talent every time. The preacher who is one hundred percent sure of his or her call might as well dedicate himself or herself to God. He or she will always be more effective than any and everybody else. Having said that, I would encourage budding preachers to study more than one preacher. Apropos in this regard is the old joke, "If you copy from one person, that's plagiarism; if you copy from a lot of people, that's research." I looked at a variety of preachers, and that helped me tremendously. Thirdly, up-and-coming preachers must know that preaching is hard work. Some young black preachers are satisfied with only capturing the sound of black preaching, not its content. The preacher who is satisfied with sound will soon be bypassed by someone who sounds better. The preacher who digs into the word will not likely be bypassed. While I believe that there are mannerisms and other stylistic features that are important to preaching, it is content that will make for the lasting effectiveness of the preacher. Eventually people will cease to listen to the preacher who sounds good but has little or nothing to say.

RCJ: Where do you see preaching going in the 21st century?

WLP: Because our society is becoming more and more diverse, black preaching, as we know it, will have to be broadened to transcend ethnic and cultural traditions. Additionally, post-modernism and secularism have conspired to make preaching much more challenging, if not difficult. By that I mean that the preacher has to preach from "ground zero," beginning with universal truths everybody embraces, not Bible truths or stories people are inclined to call into question. A new kind of contextualized preaching will be required as we get further into the 21st century, one in which we begin where the people are and not where we want them to be. John the Baptist, though a country dweller, went to the city to preach, and I am sure one reason he was effective was because he was relevant. Now as it relates to stories, because secular people still love stories, and the Bible has some of the best stories in the world, 21st century preachers will have to utilize

Bible stories more to connect with the secular mind. Ellen White reminds us that Jesus captured the imagination of His hearers with the compelling stories He told. A story will never wear itself out; it will always "gather a crowd."

The Sermon

"Called to the Dry Bones District"

"The hand of the Lord was upon me, and he brought me out by the Spirit of the Lord and set me in the middle of a valley; it was full of bones. He led me back and forth among them, and I saw a great many bones on the floor of the valley, bones that were very dry. He asked me, 'Son of man, can these bones live?' I said, 'O Sovereign Lord, you alone know. Then he said to me, 'Prophesy to these bones and say to them, 'Dry bones, hear the word of the Lord'" (Eze. 37: 1-4, NIV).

Let us pray. Father, the time is far spent and it is too late for us to be here for form or fashion. So we ask that extraneous thoughts may be removed from us, and that somehow the Spirit of God would speak to us with conciseness and clarity in ways that communicate to our hearts and to our souls. In the name of Jesus we pray, Amen.

Brother Ezekiel, the Conference Committee has asked me to discuss with you a vote that they have taken. That's how the conversation could have started. Yet it was not a conference president that was on the other end of the line. In fact, there was no line. It was the Chairman of all the boards calling; it was God Himself. Consequently, the preacher did not have the luxury of saying that the brethren had not been in touch with God. The preacher could not pass it off as a mistake made by people motivated by politics.

It was God who spoke directly to the preacher. It was God Himself who lifted the preacher from where he was, transported him to a site full of dead bones, and then, adding insult to injury, asked the preacher, "Can these bones live?" Was there any possibility? The preacher was in a predicament, and it would have been the same had he been accosted by a human personality. If the preacher answered "No," it would have seemed that he lacked faith. If he answered "Yes," it would seem that he was full of presumption. Not knowing what to say, Ezekiel, displaying much wisdom, turned the question right back to God.

Here is a preacher sent into a seemingly hopeless situation–a district full of dead folk–and God tells the preacher that he has just one option. The preacher must preach unto these dead folk. He must talk to dead people. He must communicate with dead folk. And God tells him that God's power will be able to get these folk up! When you think about it, it doesn't make sense.

Now, God has the power to communicate with the dead. The Bible makes it plain that when Christ comes again and calls to the bosom of the earth, that the dead in Christ will rise first. But how can a human being talk to dead people, telling them BEFORE they live that they will live? That's exactly what God told Ezekiel to do, to talk to dead folk.

If like me you feel that bones are inanimate, you will miss the point of this story. The fact is that bones are not supposed to be dry. I had to go to the library and pull out a few books and spread them out on a table to understand all there is to know about bones. The fact is bones are not just structural creatures; they are not just inert objects. I did a little homework on the subject that you may appreciate. I discovered that in 1691 there was a man who looked at bones and discovered that blood vessels run through bones. In 1756 another scientist discovered not one but many blood vessels flowing through bones. Then in the 19th century it became generally accepted that bones are growing mechanisms capable of producing blood.

God did not tell Ezekiel that He wanted him to understand all the intricacies of bones, however, God just told Ezekiel to talk to them. Ezekiel was admonished to speak the Word of God to the bones, and they would live. Now, all the marrow of these bones was gone; all blood production had stopped; all life had ceased. And these bones were grouped in a fashion and presented a sight that would make any preacher rethink his or her call. Yet I do not see anywhere or read anywhere in the Bible where Ezekiel said that he would not go.

I've been to districts that come perilously close to Ezekiel's district. I'll never name them. There is a preacher present here today whom I once called to my district because I thought I had lost the Holy Ghost. I used to preach my sermons in other places just to be sure they were alright. I would preach in the first church and the folk would say "Amen." I would preach the same sermon in the other church, and because I had made some improvements, the folk over there would jump up and down. Then I'd go to the third church, and the folk over there would look at me as though I'd lost my mind. And so, believing that I'd come to the end of my ministry, I decided to bring in someone who I thought still had it. Guess what? They looked at him as though he was crazy, too.

The fact is, the bones were dry. Yet we must understand that dry bones do not present an impossible situation to God. Let me say something that may come as a shock to some of you but nonetheless is very true. It is not in our province to make people live again! We are not called to bring life! We are not expected to bring life! To us God simply says: "Preach my word! Talk to the dry bones!"

We take too much unto ourselves as preachers. Some of us feel that if folk don't respond with an "Amen" something is wrong with the sermon or with us. The fact is that some sermons ought to make people quiet. We are not to preach as though life depended on us. That kind of thinking will make you go out of your mind.

Ezekiel was told to preach to the bones. And he was not to tell them what he thought. He was not to tell them what the great scholars thought. He was not to quote from Newsweek. He was not to quote from popular songs. Ezekiel was simply to preach the Word of the Lord. The result would be that he would see something happen for which he would not be responsible.

I remember when I did not make long appeals at the end of my sermons, the reason being that I took things rather personal. I got upset whenever I made an appeal and nobody came forward. I thought people would think that I did not have enough power to move people, to make people come down. I confess to you that I can hold a call now for as long as the Lord tells me to. If people come forward, praise God. If no one moves, Praise God. It is not my fault if they don't, neither is it to my glory if they do! It is the work of the Holy Ghost! The miracle of life belongs to God.

I learned something more when I looked into the matter of bones. A gentleman by the name of Clyde Snow, who is the world's most sought-after forensic anthropologist, says that given a box of bones he can tell who the individual was, what was their racial background, how old the person was, their height, approximate weight, and possibly where the person lived. It's called osteo-biography, meaning your bones will tell on you. Snow says that a narrow, steep pelvis indicates masculinity; and that a broad, shallow pelvis indicates the person was female. The ridge and nasal margins tell of the racial makeup of the individual, no matter how much plastic surgery you may have had. The cranium tells how old the person was when he or she died. The bones tell on you!

So, come with me, if you would. When God tells Ezekiel to go down to a valley of dry bones, was God not telling him to go down to a valley of stories? Was God not saying to Ezekiel that he was to go to a place where some stories ended on a sad note. In that valley the people of Israel died, leaving bones that were dried and bleached! When God looked down at that place, God did not just see a bunch of bones, but the stories of people who struggled, thinking they could make it. God saw the stories of people who expired through sad circumstances. And God wanted Ezekiel to tell those people that when all seems lost, that nothing is lost when God is there. God wanted Ezekiel to preach that God would give His people another chance.

I say to you tonight that the miracle of ministry, regardless of where you may be, is that you and I are part of a delivery system of the Word of God.

And when you think about it, we are not worthy of this responsibility. The message that we carry is so much greater than we are. It is so great that sometimes we shrink from it. Yet, the fact is that God has chosen us, just as He called Ezekiel. Think about it. God didn't have to call or use a human being. The Bible says that if we refuse to talk that one day God will make the rocks and the stones cry out. God could have told the rocks under the bones to get up! And the rocks would have spoken to the bones, and the same power that attended Ezekiel's words would have attended the words of the rocks and stones. The bones would have gotten up because of stones. But God has chosen in His mercy and in His kindness to use us, to let us have a little piece of His ministry.

I don't know about you, but I'm kinda glad about all of this. I do not want to gloss over this point. I think that some of us have been overcome with that upward mobility that is worldly. We have come to believe that because the pay scale is not what it should be, and because some places are more fertile than others, that we deserve better. We have forgotten about the dignity of the delivery system. I am convinced that if everybody else earned a million dollars a year and I was only to be given a dollar a year, the power of delivering God's Word would still be an equalizer.

I sat in the home of a friend some time ago. His words are still ringing in my ears today. Those words were, "Pastor, pray for me." The man's daughter had already informed me that he had been diagnosed with an incurable disease and that he had come home to die. There was nothing that could be done for him anymore. As we sat down, that gentleman began to talk with me about the Word. You know how it is when you know you're going to die. Yet, as you know, there is power in the Word. So when I began to quote a couple of verses of Scripture that man started to sit up a little, and when I started to share experiences of what God had done for others, that man leaned up some more. Then he began to quote Scripture and smiles began to mark his face. The end result was that we got down on our knees and I prayed for that man and his entire family. When I got through praying, the man was able to pull himself up. Discarding his walker, he escorted me to the door, and two Sabbaths later I saw him walking in church! A dead man! A dead man! God had lifted him up!

I like the way one writer captures the power of God to create and recreate. This writer says that after Jesus bent down and made the skeleton, He made the circulatory system, and the nervous system, and so forth. Then God bent down and pulled that thing up, stood it in front of Him, and put His arm around it, and breathed gently into its nostrils. Then God stepped back from it, but it did not fall! Its eyes blinked, its tongue formed words, its lips parted, its arms moved poetically, its hands motioned in the air, and it spoke to its Maker. God can make that happen. And God did not give away that ability when the six days of creation were passed. God still makes bones get up!

The fact is that some of us sit around and denigrate the power of God to speak life into seemingly hopeless situations. Just because people do not rise to their feet every Sabbath does not mean that change has not occurred.

When Ezekiel was finished with his proclamation, something happened down in the valley. It had been a rough district, a church of no "Amens." Yet when Ezekiel was through preaching, it was a transformed situation. Things must have looked awfully good and organized to Ezekiel when those bones came together. But God was not through. If Spielberg had directed the movie, all there would have been at this point would have been strange, eerie sounds. Ezekiel had to follow God's injunction to prophesy one more time. You see, these bones now looked as though they were alive, but they were still dead.

I must pause now. Maybe that is the Laodicean sickness—looking alive, but still being dead. You've got your bones, and your nerves, and your blood vessels, and your hair, and your skin, and your eyes, and your tongue, and you look like you can get up, but you cannot get up apart from the Word of God! There are churches that look like paintings of people. They are the same every Sabbath. These people have the same faces every Sabbath. They sit in the same pews every Sabbath. They have the same smirks and the same grins and the same smiles, but there is no power there. There is no life there. Ezekiel must speak again.

Ezekiel beckons the wind to come, and the same power that came out of the mouth of Jesus into the nostrils of Adam comes from God again. Where it comes from I do not know, but it blows down into the church and the members stand up. And the Bible says they became a great army. You and I have been looking for an army for a long time, but an army does not come because you tell it to come. An army does not come because you give out literature. An army does not come because you send people out. An army does not come because you put people in bands. An army does not come because people seem to be organized, or because they seem to be wealthy or healthy, or because they seem to be well-equipped, or because they seem to be well-dressed. An army comes by the Word of God!

We need to re-calculate what is important in the Seventh-day Adventist Church. I believe that part of the problem with the ministry, including the ministry of teaching and the ministry of Bible work, is that we do not think we are important anymore. The windows of heaven notwithstanding, we are all going through tough economic times. Add to this fact are those things that come down from up, and those which come from down up, and it's enough to make a preacher throw up his or hands up in despair. Yet, God's word to us is "Prophesy!"

That doesn't just mean to speak, but also to live. When we prophesy in all that we do, everybody won't be happy, but that doesn't matter. We'll be following the orders of God.

I am sobered when I think that angels want to do what I am doing. Just think about it. There are angels who would love to be in this pulpit right now. That's right, angels. That's why every now and then when I stand in the pulpit and get it right, when that power comes through me that sometimes surprises even me, I am grateful. And I know that it is the power of God, not my own power. It's about time we focus on what counts. It is not the car you drive, the clothes you wear, or even the pay scale that counts. What counts is the power that flows through you!

If you were to be made the president of the General Conference and no power flowed through you, you'd be a person most miserable. But if you could just be a humble somebody, and every now and then feel the throbbing power of the Holy Ghost coming through you, you'd be alright. You don't have to hold it; just let it flow through you. Just let it fly on by. Just feeling the power is enough.

I'm tired of a powerless religion. I'm tired of that hand-wringing, navel-watching, platitude-pushing preaching that leaves people just like we met them. It's time for us to make something happen in the pulpit, not because of us, but because of Him. So read yourself full, pray yourself hot, and let yourselves go. Your district may be on top of Mt. Carmel and your humble offerings may be on top of cold stones, Baal's prophets may tease you to weep, and circumstances may pour cold water on your plans, but look humbly up to God. Call humbly on the name of the Lord, and in the name of Jesus ask God for what you need. God will carve out a channel through the embattlements of space and send down fire and light up your sacrifice. So fall down on humble knees, reach up with faith-filled arms, cry out with a hope-moistened tongue, and God will hear you. Stop mumbling and tumbling and prophesy to the dry bones. Take hold of God with one arm and God's people with the other and let's get real with the power.

Preach like John the Baptist when they came to get him. Preach like John the Revelator, boiling in a cauldron of hot oil. Well, John wasn't boiling, the oil was boiling; John was cool! The spirit of prophecy says that God sent in the same angels that cooled off Nebuchadnezzar's furnace to cool that cauldron of boiling oil. The result was that instead of boiling John up the oil just made his skin look good! So preach like John! Preach like that.

Preach like Stephen. Though you may be in a dry-bones district, fix your eyes on Jesus and preach anyhow. They may throw stones at you, and believe me, they will, but look at Jesus standing on the right hand of God even as those stones are hitting you. Jesus may save you and He may not, but if you die looking at Jesus you've lost nothing. So prophesy. Prophesy!

So that some critic will not have much to say, I must add, before I close, that the primary application of this text had to do with Israel. Israel had come to the place where all the emblems of government had disappeared. They were in exile, without power. One scholar states that they had come to believe that if even God expelled their enemy from their land, they lacked the power to return to possess it. So Israel had lost hope. The gleam in their eyes was gone. They believed that death was better than life. They began to criticize God, believing that God had deserted them.

I've met preachers and teachers walking through life like zombies, the spark long gone from their eyes. My mother was a church school teacher in a little town in the south. Once I heard her say to a student who had lost all hope, "Boy, don't you know that there is a switch in your head? Don't you know that if you switch it on you can learn anything?" She continued, "This place may look funny, but it's just as good as Harvard, or Princeton, or Yale." A few years later I was preaching in New Jersey when an intelligent-looking man ran forward and embraced me. He told me that he had just earned his Ph.D., due in part to the encouragement of my mother. That dear soul, who is dead now, had succeeded in instilling hope in that man.

Son of man, can these bones live? O, Lord God, thou knowest.

EIGHT

Henry Monroe Wright

Henry Monroe Wright is a preacher *par excellence* who vaulted into national and international prominence shortly after accepting a teaching position in the Department of Religion and Theology at Oakwood College. Wright went on to become the president of the Allegheny West Conference of Seventh-day Adventists and secretary of the Columbia Union Conference. Currently, he is the senior/pulpit minister of the Community Praise SDA Church in Alexandria, Virginia, and an adjunct professor of preaching at Columbia Union College. Wright is known for his fresh scriptural insights, which result from in-depth Bible study. Gifted with a deep, resonate voice, which he knows how to use for maximum effect, Wright delivers his sermons with precision and power. He crafts his sermons with the accomplished writer's penchant for detail, and the result is that his messages are always clear and concise. His sermon in this volume, "Born to Triumph," was delivered at the General Conference Session in 1985. It was first printed in the *Adventist Review* and is reprinted here with the permission of the author.

The Interview

RCJ: Was preaching always your first love? Was it something you always wanted to do?

HW: Preaching was clearly not my first love. I didn't even have the desire, didn't even realize that the Lord had laid that unction on me, until my junior year at Oakwood College. Others saw the gifts of preaching in me way before I did. I did not have a Damascus Road experience. Mine was a gradual settling in. Looking back now, I recognize that I always had, even as a boy, an admiration for preaching and preachers. I can picture myself sitting under those tents at the old Allegheny Camp Meeting listening to men like E. E. Cleveland and Jacob Justiss and Wagner and DeShay. As an 8- and 9-year-old, I sat and listened in rapt attention without realizing that the call to preach was on me.

RCJ: Who were some of the preachers you admired and perhaps tried to emulate in your early preaching career? Were the men you just mentioned included in the list?

HW: Jacob Justiss comes to mind first. He was my pastor. Justiss was a historical preacher, perhaps because he was a trained historian before he entered the pastoral ministry. I've always like the historical element or aspect to preaching. I also admired Aaron Brogden. He was erudite, articulate, and very mental in his preaching. The verbal eloquence of C. D. Brooks, with whom I worked one summer; and the powerful, dynamite style of J. Malcolm Phipps, with whom I worked a couple of summers, are a couple of other names that come to mind. These individuals had an impact on me, not so such because of their style, but because of their content, language, and deportment in the pulpit. I cannot say that I ever tried to mimic the style of any of them, but I certainly admired their content and the order of their material. I tried to emulate that. I must also add the name of Calvin Rock, whom I did not hear until after entering the ministry. I admired his studied, developmental style, and the progression of thought that I saw in him and that he still possesses.

RCJ: What is your theology of preaching, and how do you define a sermon?

HW: Preaching is God's Word manifested in human personality for the purpose of touching other human personalities. And this is why I resist the idea or practice of copying. If the Lord wanted everyone to sound like a C. D. Brooks or a Walter Pearson or a Cliff Jones, the Lord would have called just those people. The unique majesty of preaching is that God's Word can manifest itself dynamically and powerfully in any human personality that has been anointed by God. Building on that understanding or definition, the sermon then becomes God's Word as sifted through the preacher's experience. That's one reason why two preachers will preach two completely different sermons on the same scriptural passage. A sermon is like a photograph of the impact of a particular passage of Scripture on my life at a particular time and place. If I were to return to that same passage ten years down the road, chances are I'll preach a different sermon. This truth makes a sermon a rare document that captures what God is doing in me at a particular moment in time.

RCJ: I've heard preachers talk about the agony and the ecstasy of preaching? What do you think is meant by this? What is the agony and the ecstasy of preaching?

HW: The agony of preaching is manifested in three ways. First, the preacher does not mount the pulpit without a deep consciousness that he or she is part of the problem about which he or she is about to preach. Second, preachers preach to people who very often know as much or sometimes even more about the Word than the preachers do. The preacher is the one preaching, but he or she is not necessarily the one who knows the most about the Word. Third, we preachers will ever be preaching on a subject that will always be beyond us—God, God's salvation, God's character. If you write 10,000 sermons, they will only cover a pin head of who God is. That is the triple agony of preaching. The ecstasy of preaching may be summed up in the thought or realization that whether you're preaching to a group of dormitory students or to 40,000 people as I did in the New Orleans Superdome at the General Conference Session in 1985, that God would use you to alter lives and to light up faces. And it's sobering that God allows us to savor this time after time after time.

RCJ: How do you prepare your sermons? What's you step-by-step approach? How much reading do you do, and what do you read? When and which commentaries do you consult?

HW: Having taught Homiletics, I've pretty much honed down an approach. Basically, I have eight steps. These steps are shared with the assumption that I am constantly reading the Bible, theological works, professional material, and magazines covering current events. That's one assumption that goes along with my eight-step method. Another assumption, of course, is that I am leading a life of prayer and consulting with God. Given those two assumptions, my first step is to select the passage, reading it in as many versions as possible. While I read, I jot down my first impressions. I call this the brooding process. Order is not important in this step; I'm just putting down on paper the thoughts that are flooding my mind as I read the passage. I may take up to two hours doing this, just mulling over the passage. In step two, I begin to look at key words. This is where my facility with Greek and Hebrew come into play. In this step, my objective is to get as close to the original situation as I can. I try to answer questions such as who is writing, to whom is this passage directed, and what prompted the words of the passage. I am searching for intent, acutely aware that you cannot go forward until you've gone backward to the passage. This is a very lengthy step because I consult several commentaries, including the SDA Commentary and Bible dictionaries for help.

RCJ: What are the other steps?

HW: In step three, I try to hammer out a theme statement. Where am I going with this passage? What am I trying to accomplish with it? Those are crucial questions at this juncture. As you know, a verse of the Bible can sometimes give you as many as five different directions. In crafting a thesis statement, I ask myself, "To whom am I talking?" and "What's the occasion?" Illustrative material is what step four is all about. I need windows to help people see where I am going. My favorite source of illustrations is *Reader's Digest* because I like current and real-life material. I also look for illustrations in the world of science, the reason being that because I once thought science was my calling I am still intrigued by the world of science. In step five I start writing, and because I am a manuscript preacher I put everything down word for word. I firmly believe that preachers must preserve their encounters with God, which is what every sermon preparation moment is. Because God has blessed me with a fairly good memory, I really do not need to preach from a manuscript, but nine times out of ten the manuscript will go into the pulpit with me.

RCJ: What is step six?

HW: In step six I start anticipating the appeal. I must admit that the ending of the sermon is for me the most difficult part of the sermon, one reason being that you must go back and try to ascertain that you've covered the bases. I tell my students that they must not raise conundrums or issues they're not prepared to answer in their sermons, and that they must resolve each and every issue they raise. In the conclusion, I try to pull all the loose ends together. In step seven, I deal with something I call my measuring rod. I ask myself, Does the sermon have continuity? Does the sermon have movement? Does the sermon have unity of thought? Does the sermon possess the golden chord of purpose? And does the sermon have a point of intersection? In other words, at what point in the sermon does man's path and God's path intersect? Because the purpose of preaching is to turn people around, there must be a clear point where man and God face each other and man emerges from the encounter submissive.

RCJ: What's your eighth and final step?

HW: My last step, believe it or not, is that, after all these years, I rehearse. I rehearse by reading the sermon out loud because it is in so doing that I am able to answer the questions I pose as part of my measuring rod. I often use a tape recorder to help in the exercise, knowing that a tape recorder does not lie. When she is available, I use my wife, tapping into her phlegmatic personality. She is a good critic who has a benign way of letting me know where I need to improve.

RCJ: Earlier, you mentioned that you prepare a manuscript. How much of your written material do you take into the pulpit with you? And do you think that manuscript preaching detracts from your effectiveness?

HW: Preaching from a manuscript does not detract from my effectiveness. I had a good role model in this regard, perhaps the most effective manuscript preacher I have ever known-C. D. Brooks. Most people don't know that everything C. D. says in the pulpit is written down on a stack of paper before him. I was shocked when I discovered this as a young man working for C. D., who even then was known as an erudite, articulate preacher. Now, not everybody can preach effectively from a manuscript. For example, I don't see a Walter Pearson doing that; Walter is a soul that must fly free. I must add that I never preach from a manuscript just as it is written. My manuscripts are guides that keep me focused and directed, and within my time parameters.

RCJ: Which person, book, experience, or commentary has had the most telling impact on your preaching?

HW: No one person, book, or commentary has had that kind of impact on my preaching, and I say that kindly. To be sure, I do a lot of reading, and I find one of your colleagues at the Seminary, George Knight, to be particularly informative and interesting. I also love E. M. Bounds because of the emphasis he places on the preacher's spirituality, and although I do not always agree with Philip Yancey, I also like what he writes.

RCJ: What's your most important concern when you enter the pulpit?

HW: Clarity is my most important concern. I tell my students over and over that if they must sacrifice anything, they must never sacrifice clarity. Be clear, make sense. People who have worked hard all week deserve, at the very least, a sermon that is clear. I feel as though I have been crushed by a bulldozer when my wife says to me that I did not make sense.

RCJ: What role do you think revelation and inspiration have in preaching?

HW: It is the revelation of God through the individuals who penned the words of Scripture that must be preached, and any inspiration that comes to the preacher as he or she prepares that sermon must be gauged by that original Word. We preachers must seek to ascertain that we are only interpreting the Word as best as we can. Inspiration must be a clear, valid documentation of what God has said in God's Word. It is critical that this happen lest the preacher's interpretation of that Word become his or her god. Ultimately, we preach the Word, not Henry, not Cliff; we preach the word. That's one reason the second of my eight steps of sermon preparation is so vital.

RCJ: How do you capture and maintain the attention and interest of your hearers?

HW: First, your introduction must be verbally astute and catchy, and must speak to some immediacy in the experience of your hearers. Those first sentences are crucial. Hopefully, they'll be provocative and well-thought-out and be some of the best in the sermon, and they must be uttered as you establish eye contact with your audience. Another tactic that I use to capture and maintain attention and interest is that of calling people's names. What this strategy says to people is that I am talking to them, that I am focused on them. Throughout the sermon I use questions, pauses, and the interactive strategy of having the people read something that I may have distributed or from the Bible to keep them aboard. The bottom line is that I must appeal to the four people types—the phlegmatic, the melancholy, the sanguine, and the choleric—and it takes much for each of the quadrants of the brain to remained engaged. If I am lucky, I may have 50 percent of the audience with me at the end.

RCJ: What is the toughest part of the sermon for you to prepare and preach; conversely, what is the easiest part?

HW: The easiest part is the introduction. I like introductions, and when I am in the audience I like to listen to see how preachers get going. I think my introductions are usually the strongest part of my sermons. I have to work on my conclusions, and on occasions I have entered the pulpit unsure of my conclusion. Maybe the Lord has fixed it so to keep me humble. When I have entered the pulpit uncertain of how I am going to end, just trusting in the Lord to help, God has come through for me. Interestingly, I've noted that many people do not begin to listen until you begin to wrap up, making recapitulation and summarizing vitally important.

RCJ: You are known for, among other things, your timing, pacing, diction, vivid imagination and use of words. How did you develop and cultivate these traits?

HW: You're very kind. I have worked hard at anything for which I may be known. The diction comes from being reared by a mother of Jamaican extraction who tolerated no slovenly speech in her house. Because you did not talk lazily around my mother, I developed the art of speaking clearly very early in life. My timing is an answer to my greatest weakness in the pulpit, even though I still struggle with speaking way too fast. I have had to work at slowing down, at using the pause, at deliberate pronunciation and enunciation. As it relates to language, I was one of those many young preachers who grew up admiring C. D. Brooks, who, incidentally, just concluded a Week of Prayer for me and is, as far as I am concerned, one of the most gifted speakers I know. As I sat and listened to C. D., I found myself saying more than once, "If I could just say it like that." Erudite language rolls off the lips of Elder Brooks like water pours over Niagara Falls. This is another reason I write out my sermons. As you know, writing develops proficiency in the use of language.

RCJ: You are ranked among the most gifted Seventh-day Adventist preachers. What makes for your effectiveness?

HW: Given the agreed assumption that I do not ascribe to that view, I will say that a key may be found in something I often hear people, especially my members, say after I have preached. I have had people tell me that what draws them to my preaching is that I seem to care and that I appear natural in the pulpit. One thing I can say about my preaching is that I have never, even as a young preacher, tried to mimic someone in the pulpit. I really believe in letting my personality flow. As to my effectiveness, I do think that I have developed a facility for language that may appeal to people.

RCJ: What are your weak areas? In other words, where do you still need to grow as a preacher?

HW: I still talk too fast sometimes. That's my biggest weakness. In addition, I do not always have an appealing tone in my voice. Because of my lung disease I sometimes get dry, a fact that makes for shrillness. My wife tells me that I sometimes get a tad too humorous in the pulpit. It's a subject we do not agree on. My melancholy-choleric personality, the lower left quadrant, makes for shyness and the organizing principle on my part. Pushed into the pulpit by God, things come out of me that aren't naturally there.

RCJ: In what ways have preaching changed since you started preaching?

HW: Preaching styles have not changed much from what they used to be when I started preaching forty years ago, except that modern preachers seem to have a greater facility in terms of applying the Word to their times. Preachers of yesteryear were very biblical and often implicit as far as applying the message of Scripture to their context was concerned. Not so with preachers of today, who are quite adept at what I call the hands-on approach. It's a sort of "how to tune up your car" kind of preaching. This trend fits with the make up of today's society, which is very hands-on. Sermons have become more relational in terms of content, too. There is more preaching about getting along with each other, about getting along with your family, about getting along with your fellow man. There is less proclamatory preaching about the doctrines, and in many circles there is a steering away from the doctrines altogether. A consequence of this trend is that there is a kind of barrenness in the pulpit. We need those "thus saiths" as much as we need the "how to's"

RCJ: To follow up, what do you think is the future of preaching?

HW: One of the most important and one of the most positive trends is that preachers are doing more teaching than preaching in the pulpit. As you know, in the book *Gospel Workers* Ellen White makes much of the importance of teaching. My own preaching style as a pastor-preacher at Community Praise Fellowship Church is as much a teaching kind of presentation as it is a declaration-proclamation kind of presentation. I love to see people with their Bibles opened in their laps, and I relish the sound of turning pages as people search the Word of God. This current trend in preaching may indicate that pulpiteering as we know it may very well fade. Another reality which is impacting preaching is the video consciousness of the present generation. Sights, sounds, color, and movement are all important to this generation, who may only come to hear the preacher when power point presentations are taking place. If the Lord delays His coming for another couple of generations, technology may be the dominant factor in preaching, and I say this with neither fear nor concern.

RCJ: Much ado has been made about black preaching. Please comment on the genre?

HW: I am both a believer in and not a believer in black preaching. I understand the use of the term, and I am fully aware of the assumption that black preachers deliver the Word with more dynamism and color and do more story telling than their white counterparts, who, allegedly, do more benign preaching. Yet what is forgotten in that assumption is that black preachers learned to preach from white preachers. We were slaves who were brought to America in ships, and we listened to white preachers first. Now, what kind of preaching did the majority of those white preachers do? It was not the lectern-style type of preaching that we associate with today's white preachers, but the powerful preaching of men like Jonathan Edwards. In that sense, black preaching has preserved something that others need to rediscover.

RCJ: Anything else about black preaching?

HW: We know that the black style of preaching, which was honed in the cotton fields, was a kind of story-telling, incisive, highly descriptive painting of the Bible that was necessary for a people who could not read the Bible for themselves. As such, there was a necessity that called for black preaching. Yet early black preachers learned the craft from white men.

RCJ: What are your views about celebration in preaching?

HW: I have no problem with celebration, firmly believing that celebration is vital to every aspect of worship. Without celebration, worship falls short. In the book of Leviticus it is God who says, "Celebrate my sabbaths." To whom is God talking? Freed slaves. Preaching that does not cut loose and celebrate at some point is deficient. Celebration is legitimate, real, and vital.

RCJ: **What counsel do you have for young preachers? What are some of the disciplines they should cultivate and practice, and what are some of the pitfalls they should avoid?**

HW: Number one, they should read. It goes without saying that their book of first choice should be the Bible. Yet they should also read broadly. I am a firm believer that good preaching grows out of good reading. Secondly, preachers should become adept and adroit at writing, learning how to describe what they are thinking. They should become competent at linking adjectives with nouns, adverbs with verbs, and using conjunctions that either continue or intersect action. Proficiency at putting down one's thoughts is a skill that pays rich dividends. If there is anything a young preacher should avoid, it is that of becoming a copycat. Believe that if God called you God saw some skills and talents in you that God can develop and use to God's glory. So develop those. Another thing I say to young preachers all the time is that the best way they can develop their preaching is by preaching. As such, they should respond to opportunities to preach in the affirmative, even when they feel they are not up to their best. All that I have said is based on the assumption that the preacher is developing as a person of prayer and has a passionate love for God and God's people.

The Sermon

"Born to Triumph"

"**After this I looked, and behold, a great multitude which no man could number, from every nation, from all tribes and peoples and tongues, standing before the throne and before the Lamb**" (Rev. 7:9 RSV).

Revelation 7:9 is many millennia and countless billions of heartbeats from the sublime arena of Eden. Nobody will understand that better than Adam. Can you picture him who, shaped by the very hand of the Creator, rises to focus his unblurring optics upon the face of Him who is ever lovely? His mind is clear and instantly intelligent; his huge frame quakes from no infirmity. Luke records in his paternal genealogy of Jesus that Adam was "the son of God". In his heart beat no desire for sin. He was born to triumph!

"Adam was crowned as king in Eden. To him was given dominion over every living thing God had created. The Lord blessed Adam and Eve with intelligence such as He had not given to the animal creation."—*Review and Herald*, Feb. 24, 1874.

"Then the Lord God said, 'It is not good that the man should be alone; I will make him a helper fit for him.' . . . So the Lord God caused a deep sleep to fall upon the man, and while he slept took one of his ribs and closed up its place with flesh; and the rib which the Lord God had taken from the man he made into a woman and brought her to the man" (Gen. 2:18-22).

As angels beheld this holy pair—these two made for one another, these two (one bearing the sterner virtues of God, and the other the softer attributes of divinity) holding hands and looking into one another's eyes, he male, she female—the sons of God shouted for joy; the heavens declared God's triumph.

"God created man for His own glory, that after test and trial the human family might become one with the heavenly family. It was God's purpose to repopulate heaven with the human family, if they would show themselves obedient to His every word. . . . If he (Adam) stood the test, his instruction to his children would have been only of loyalty. His mind and thoughts would have been as the mind and thoughts of God."—Ellen G. White, *The SDA Bible Commentary*, vol. 1, p. 1082.

Oh, yes! Man was born to triumph!

But the scene changes. A voice, yes, the voice of the Creator, is saying to the woman, "I will greatly multiply your pain in childrearing; in pain you shall bring forth children" (chap. 3:16). Adam and Eve are now clothed in garments of defeat and selfishness. That same voice, as commanding as thunder's distant rumbling, has just addressed the author of rebellion: "I will put enmity between you and the woman, and between your seed and her seed; he shall bruise your head, and you shall bruise his heel" (verse 15).

The Creator's voice, which had exultantly declared, "Let us make man in our image, after our likeness" (chap. 1:26), now with gentle tones turns to Adam, His son. The voice is pregnant with grief that only one who loves divinely can know. Here is the record: "Because you have listened to the voice of your wife, and have eaten of the tree of which I commanded you, 'You shall not eat of it,' cursed is the ground because of you; in toil you shall eat of it all the days of your life; thorns and thistles it shall bring forth to you; and you shall eat the plants of the field. In the sweat of your face you shall eat bread till you return to the ground, for out of it you were taken; you are dust, and to dust you shall return" (chap. 3:17-19). Born to triumph?

I doubt that Adam and Eve could really understand or truly listen to the words that marched across the pathway of their headlong rush to oblivion. So much was lost, so suddenly, so completely. They could not at that time grasp the stubbornness of God's love. Paul had not yet written man's bill of rights, which reads, "But God shows his love for us in that while we were yet sinners Christ died for us" (Rom. 5:8)

Handkerchief of grace

For you see, beloved, Genesis 3:15 is the John 3:16 of the Old Testament. Both promise that what is not yet, already is; that the future has swallowed the present; that hope for what will be can become peace because of what has happened. The lamb is slain from the foundation of the world. The handkerchief of Calvary's grace wipes the tears of Eden's shame.

An angel of light slammed the door of Eden. Adam and Eve had to now believe in triumph. It was not easy. Adam lived to be 930 years old. "And for hundreds of years there were seven generations living upon the earth contemporaneously."—*Patriarchs and Prophets*, p. 83.

What did Adam see? There is that sad day of anguish when he and his wife discover the blood-stained body of Abel. Feel the sorrow of this mother of all living as she cradles the lifeless head of her son.

Then Cain goes forth and builds a city. Adam could only guess that this first city would grandsire all the great cities of our day, which have become places where men pile themselves together in cesspools of numbers, where poverty, crime, sensuality, greed, and injustice reign with unbounded devastation.

Hear, my fellow believers, Adam and Eve as they in shock discuss the immortality of Cain's descendants. Cain's great-great-grandson Lamech has taken *two* wives, breaking the sacred arithmetic that said two would be one. And what about that month or year—was it hundreds of years later?—when Adam, walking among the trees and woods of skyscraper height, may have stumbled upon two of his young descendants engaging in premarital sex. But more than anything, more than all the pain of seeing sin, was the inescapable daily reminder that every act of sin, every lie told, every withering rose, oh yes, my friend, every falling leaf, was birthed in the womb of rebellion of him and his wife. Born to triumph? Triumph was hard to believe.

Adam was born to triumph, but owing to the cancer of self-reliance, his descendants were born in sin. Death, defeat, fell on all. Thus Adam and Eve's children, from the darkest of us to the whitest of us, from the richest of us to the poorest of us, from the most intelligent to the helpless imbecile, are enfeebled with defeatism. But at the same tree of the knowledge of good and evil, where the lamb of harmony and peace was devoured by the lion of disharmony and hopelessness, there was planted in man enmity, hostility, uncomfortableness, with his state.

The danger of the church is to reject that inner compass—articulated by the Holy Spirit, who pricks the conscience—that says something is wrong just when everyone is saying that it is all right. It is a drawing toward victory and an impatience with defeat.

God's move toward triumph

When Adam was 130 years old Seth was born. Seth's name means "appointed." God began to manifest His move toward our race's ultimate triumph. The record says, "To Seth also a son was born, and he called his name Enosh. At that time men began to call upon the name of the Lord" (Gen. 4:26).

This must have lifted the hearts of Adam and Eve. Eve had in hope called Cain "One Acquired." She hoped Cain was one acquired from the Lord to be that Seed who would triumph. This hope was to be buried in disappointment. Thus when Seth was born he was called "Appointed." Perhaps this was the Chosen One. The great truths given Adam and his wife, taught to them by angels—the truths of creation, Trinity, Sabbath, law, marriage, stewardship, temperance, righteousness by faith in the promise God—not only were now believed by some of their children, but now, through Seth's descendants, were taught in worship.

Adam, when he was more than 600 years old, heard the preaching of Enoch, a message of optimism, victory, and triumph. In a world losing its grip on true godliness, a world that Paul describes as reprobate and so distorted that men forgot how to be men, and women disdained true femininity—in this world Enoch began to turn the tide from defeat to victory.

"Enoch was a man of a strong and highly cultivated mind and extensive knowledge; he was honored with special revelations from God. . . . In prophetic vision he was instructed concerning the death of Christ, and was shown His coming in glory, attended by all the holy angels, to ransom His people from the grave. . . . Enoch became a preacher of righteousness. . . . Those who feared the Lord sought out this holy man, to share his instruction and his prayers."—*Patriarchs and Prophets*, pp. 85, 86.

It is possible that Adam and Eve sat with rapt attention at the preaching of this godly young man, who, inspired by becoming a father, sought out God the Father and then His earthly grandfather, seven times removed, for wisdom and direction. Can't you see Eve brush away a tear as Enoch makes an appeal to the wicked antidiluvians? Can't you rejoice with them as a few, just a few, break from the throng and take their stand for triumph? Oh, yes, my friends, I know that later only eight would be saved in the ark by the preaching of Enoch's great-grandson Noah, but some died in the faith before the ark took its stormy ride. Some of these were converted by Enoch. "I will put enmity." Triumph is our destiny!

God understands how narcotic and disorienting sin can be as this church, growing by 1,000 members a day, fights off the disarming effects of many cultures and varying social mores. We must not despair if in all the world this remnant gospel is not practiced in every place in exactly the same way. That galling enmity—that hostility against evil—when prodded develops a sense that something is not right. God will bring us together, but woe unto us, whether in South America or Korea, when we twist the gospel to meet our own weakness. Adam was born to triumph, but Adam's descendants are born in sin. Through the Seed of Adam, the Word made flesh, we are now again able to be called the sons of God, *reborn* to triumph.

Adam died not having received the promise. No one could forget as long as Adam was alive that man was born to triumph. Within less than four generations after Adam's death, only eight human beings would be alive. The waters lap over the bloated carcasses of the sons and daughters of the race. The creaking of the ark shouts out above the trumpeting of elephants, the braying of donkeys. Where is the triumph, Noah?

Prophets could hardly keep silent. Jacob said, "The scepter shall not depart from Judah, nor the ruler's staff from between his feet, until he comes to whom it belongs" (Gen. 49:10). Moses, foreseeing the triumphant Seed, said, "I will raise up for them a prophet like you from among their brethren; and I will put my words in his mouth" (Deut. 18:18). Joshua was given a glimpse of the triumphant nature of the Seed of the woman when he beheld the Captain of the Lord's host standing shod for the victorious charge against the enemy.

After the flood, man in every age struggled to believe in triumph. God dared to select a people and make them the stewards of His Word, but His Word did not appear to triumph in them. The prophets were relentless in describing the moral defeat of Adam's sons and daughters, but just as positive and consistent in declaring the triumph. Often these prophets spoke their optimism right in the face of events and situations so diametrically opposed to triumph as to make them appear to be babbling fools.

Sin more popular than salvation

How can you dare speak, Isaiah, knowing that in your day sin has become more popular than salvation? Rulers bow down to the idols of stone, metal, and wood. The temple is forsaken for personal pursuits. How can you dare write the following words?

"The wilderness and the solitary place shall be glad for them; and the desert shall rejoice, and blossom as the rose. It shall blossom abundantly, and rejoice even with joy and singing; the glory of Lebanon shall be given unto it, the excellency of Carmel and Sharon, they shall see the glory of the Lord, and the excellency of our God.

"Strengthen ye the weak hands, and confirm the feeble knees. Say to them that are of a fearful heart, Be strong, fear not: behold, your God will come with vengeance, even God with a recompence; he will come and save you.

"Then the eyes of the blind shall be opened, and the ears of the deaf shall be unstopped. Then shall the lame man leap as an hart, and the tongue of the dumb sing; for in the wilderness shall waters break out, and streams in the desert. And the parched ground shall become a pool, and the thirsty land springs of water; in the habitation of dragons, where each lay, shall be grass with reeds and rushes.

"And an highway shall be there, and a way, and it shall be called The way of holiness; the unclean shall not pass over it; but it shall be for those: the wayfaring men, though fools, shall not err therein. No lion shall be here, nor any ravenous beast shall go up thereon, it shall not be found there; but the redeemed shall walk there; and the ransomed of the Lord shall return, and come to Zion with songs and everlasting joy upon their heads; they shall obtain joy and gladness, and sorrow and sighing shall flee away." (Isa: 35, K.J.V).

Jeremiah stands at the door of a Temple where worship is more form than Spirit. His leaders and fellow believers would rather hear lies than truth. There is leadership who hears the word of the Lord and, according to Jeremiah 26, seeks to destroy the bearer of that word; but in that setting, where apostasy is on the ascendancy and pure and holy religion is addressed as fanaticism, Jeremiah is able to say: "Then I will gather the remnant of my flock out of all the countries where I have driven them, and I will bring them back to their fold, and they shall be fruitful and multiply. I will set shepherds over them who will care for them, and they shall fear no more, nor be dismayed, neither shall any be missing, says the Lord. Behold, the days are coming, says the Lord, when I will raise up for David a righteous Branch, and he shall reign as king and deal wisely, and shall execute justice and righteousness in the land. In his days Judah will be saved, and Israel will dwell securely" (chap. 23:3-6).

When I was 18 years old I read a book one summer. It begins simply enough—the two are indescribably handsome and beautiful to behold. Their relationship is sealed in love and mutual adoration. But the days of bliss are short-lived, and by the third chapter of the book a villain appears and gains the ascendancy. By the sixth chapter the original pair is dead and their children are corrupt, and by the ninth chapter a pitiful few survive. By the time I was in Exodus the hero's children are slaves, and in Numbers, though free, they are awfully ignorant, and by Joshua they are woefully inconsistent. In the end of Judges everyone does what is right in his own eyes, and by the time I finished the books of the kings, the people are bereft of their homeland, hopelessly scattered and captive in a strange land. Their prophets scold them, and their leaders desert them. It was quite an adventure!

Suddenly temptation possessed me. (I had never read the Bible before.) I desperately wanted to know, Is there triumph?

I went to the back of the Book. There were dragons, beasts, scorpions, falling stars, and symbols of all kinds; and then I saw them—obviously descendants of the original pair. They were dressed in white with palms in their hands. I could see golden crowns bedecking their heads, and yes, hear the singing—oh, what singing! As I beheld more closely in my imagination, as I read these precious chapters, I could see yellow, black, reddish, and while skin! I could see that they came from many places. The Book said they came from every nation, kindred, tongue, and people. And what a place they were in! Light was everywhere. Everyone looked well and whole. The Book said no pain, no tears, no sorrow, no death. The Book showed a big tree, the same one in the beginning of the saga. A tree called life. They sang a song. The Book said they had washed their robes in the blood of the Lamb! I could, in my imagination, feel the triumph!

I went back to an earlier part of the Book. It said, "He came unto his own, and his own received him not" (John 1:11 KJV). But I wasn't worried now; I had looked at the last chapters. I know now that through the shed blood of the Son of Adam, Son of God, I am born, yes, reborn, to triumph!

NINE

Hyveth Williams

Hyveth Williams holds a doctorate in preaching and was mentored by one of the giants in the field, William Willimon. She is one of a handful of women pastors in the United States, and commands a following because of her candor, warmth, and, not surprisingly, ability to preach. If preaching is part exposition of the Word of God and part personal testimony, then Williams preaches a full, rounded message each time she mounts the pulpit. Her story is captivating and compelling, and always told with passion and pathos. Williams is seldom received as a woman preacher, or even as a preacher who happens to be a woman. Almost always, she is viewed only as a preacher, and she delivers her sermons with the same flair and skill for which African American male preachers are known. As one who has studied preaching in depth, she is well acquainted with its mandate, means, and methodology.

The Interview

RCJ: What led to your decision to be a preacher?
HW: My call to the preaching ministry was very primitive. I was an atheist who became a Christian through a dramatic experience that time will not allow me to tell. Anyway, I thought that becoming a Christian meant that I had to tell my conversion story, so I began doing just that. Within a year, the Lord impressed upon me that I should go to college to prepare for the ministry. Public speaking was not new to me, the reason being that as an executive assistant to the mayor of the city of Hartford, Connecticut, part of my responsibilities was to speak on his behalf. Additionally, I had had a radio program that was very popular with listeners. So again, public speaking was a normal part of my life. Still, I enrolled at Columbia Union College to train to be a missionary, ignoring the call to preach. But a few of my

teachers realized that I was gifted in this respect and began to nurture, nourish, and nudge me toward the preaching ministry. Pretty soon I was preaching in local churches, which sort of confirmed my call.

RCJ: What are some of the challenges and the advantages to being a woman preacher?

HW: I would rather think of myself as a preacher woman, believing that there is a subtle difference between being a preacher woman and a woman preacher. There are women who preach, and there are preachers who happen to be women. I like to distinguish myself as a preacher who is a woman. Now to answer your question. Do you know that there have been times when I was physically attacked?

RCJ: Is that right? Were you attacked because you happened to be a preacher woman, as you put it, or because of something you may have said in the pulpit?

HW: Both. On one occasion I was attacked by a woman who was, for the most part, a legalist with very low self-esteem.

RCJ: As a preacher woman in the Seventh-day Adventist Church, what question are you most frequently asked?

HW: The question I get asked most frequently is, "How did you do it?" The answer to that is, truthfully, I didn't. I am more of a "being" Christian than a "doing" Christian anyway. If I do anything, it is to believe God and totally surrender to Him. I do not have a formula for anything I do in the pulpit.

RCJ: Who were some of the preachers you admired in your early preaching ministry?

HW: There were few preacher women in the Adventist church for me to admire when I started. In fact, I was the first black female pastor in our denomination. There were other black women who preached before me, but I was the first one hired as a pastor. So, there were no models, no models, for me, and it was a time of painful struggle for women in ministry when I came along. I did admire Barbara Jordan, the congresswoman from Texas, whom, as I recall, gave a very moving speech that shook the nation at the impeachment hearing of President Richard Nixon. I studied Jordan's use of language and speaking style, and read everything she wrote. I followed her and watched her demeanor, and was enthralled with her oral presentations. She commanded the attention of everyone when she walked into a room, and held their attention when she spoke. I concluded I wanted to be like her when I grew up.

RCJ: Was there anyone else?

HW: Jordan influenced me from the delivery aspect; from the preaching aspect, Chuck Swindoll did. I love the way Swindoll is able to tell stories and break down a passage of Scripture.

RCJ: What is your personal theology of preaching, and how do you conceive of and define a sermon?

HW: I believe that a preacher's responsibility is to be the mouth piece of God. He or she must be a prophet, which has a two-fold manifestation. Foretelling is part of the gift and is the ability to look into the future and declare what is going to happen. I do not believe I have that part of the gift, but I do believe that I have the second part of the gift, which is forthtelling. My philosophy is that as a prophet of God, as a mouthpiece of God, I speak with the power and authority of God whenever I stand in the pulpit. I speak with confidence to God's people, prodigals and others who need to be reconciled to God.

RCJ: How do you prepare your sermons? What is your step-by-step approach?

HW: I speak twice on Sabbaths at my church, delivering two different sermons at these services. I do this deliberately because before I became a Christian, and before I entered politics, I was an actress. It is very tempting for me to lapse into the acting mode, and this temptation is particularly powerful if I preach the same sermon again. This is one reason I preach a fresh sermon to each group. I want to be authentic; I do not want to be up there performing. If I am moved to tears in my first delivery, I do not want to contrive the tears for my second sermon. What do I do to prepare?

RCJ: Yes, please share how you prepare?

HW: I use the common lectionary, which follows the Christian year. With it, I am able to project three and six months down the road, something that my musicians, worship leaders, and worship participants appreciate very much. Amazingly, even with this kind of long range planning I am still able to remain current with my preaching. One benefit of a preaching calendar is that with it I am able to plan my reading. Sometimes I am able to read as many as ten books to get the right illustrations and ideas for a sermon. When I preach from the New Testament, which is often, I read the passage in the original Greek to make sure that what the author intended to convey is what I do. Usually, I spend several weeks researching a sermon, which means that there are usually three to four sermons cooking in my mind. I put the sermon on paper the night before I am to preach it, getting up at 2 o'clock Sabbath morning to write out the sermon word for word. After writing out the sermon, I summarize it into an outline, which is what I take into the pulpit. I no longer preach from a full manuscript.

RCJ: At what time do you go back to bed?

HW: I do not go back to bed.

RCJ: That means you've been up from approximately 2 a.m. when you preach on Sabbaths.

HW: My body has adjusted to this routine. I do try to get to bed by 9 o'clock on Friday nights.

RCJ: Do you wish to add anything about your preparation routine?

HW: Earlier I mentioned that I might read as many as ten books for any one sermon. I include biographies and autobiographies, believing that they are excellent sources for illustrations, and I read plays by Shakespeare. Studying excites me, and I've been studious all my life. I read magazines on airplanes, everything from *People* magazine to *Time* magazine. I may not quote anything from these sources, but I believe reading them helps me be a better spokesperson for God. I try to stay away from internet illustrations, because I've found that half way through them the congregation will finish them for you. One last thing. I have learned that diligence in my personal devotional life pays rich dividends. In fact, preparing oneself to preach is as important if not more important than preparing the sermon itself.

RCJ: Which is the most difficult part of the preparation process?

HW: Deciding what to use and what to discard. After weeks of reading, I'm usually inundated with so much material that deciding what to put into the forty-five minutes I'll be speaking is a challenge.

RCJ: Good writing and good preaching. What is the relationship?

HW: Good preaching cannot exist without good writing. Good writing implies that the preacher uses imagination and humor to paint word pictures in the minds of people. As someone has said, good preaching is having a conversation with God and God's people. One has to be able to put all the thoughts of that conversation together so that it flows smoothly and the congregation remains engaged. That's one reason I write out my sermons word for word. I want to be sure that grammatically I'm correct and precise.

RCJ: You are a church pastor. Do you do series preaching?

HW: I am doing more and more of that. I just finished a seven-part Easter series entitled, "Countdown to the Cross." It ended with the seven last words of Christ being performed by my choir. Currently, I am in the middle of a six-part series from Ephesians called, "The Portrait of Christ's Church." After this, I plan to do a series on the Sabbath.

RCJ: Which spiritual disciplines do you practice in preparation for preaching, and how much time do you spend in these exercises?

HW: Because study, prayer, and fasting were all new to me when I became a Christian, I can recall rather accurately what I was doing and how much time I was spending doing it. Now, these spiritual disciplines are so much a part of me that it is difficult for me to quantify them. They come naturally. I am constantly in prayer, asking for God's guidance and wisdom because I realize God has been dealing all week long with the people to whom I'll be speaking for approximately forty minutes. I need God's influence if I'm going to be effective.

RCJ: Why do you think you are considered one of Adventism's outstanding preachers?

HW: I do not know why I've been given that appellation. Looking at myself from the backside of the pulpit, I see a nervous individual, someone who is afraid she might say something that may drive someone from God for ever. Consequently, I experience the preaching moment with a reverence that is uncharacteristic for my sanguine nature. Preaching is an awesome responsibility and opportunity to which I have not as yet gotten used. To think that God has chosen to speak through me is truly sobering.

RCJ: Is there anything about you that sets you apart?

HW: If anything, it is my ability to tell stories. My grandmother was a great storyteller, and I inherited the skill from her. Research shows that women are great storytellers and bring to narrative preaching an almost natural ability. I love words. I enjoy seeing words take on a life of their own. I love to paint with words.

RCJ: Are you more of a narrative preacher then? Or are you generally a topical, textual, or expository preacher?

HW: I am all of the above, utilizing every one of them to the fullest. As you know, it all depends on the pericope, the preaching portion.

RCJ: Do you rehearse your sermons? If not, how do you critique yourself?

HW: My voice was very weak when I started preaching. Friends would nag me to death about my voice, wondering what the problem was. I read that Ellen White had a similar problem and that she practiced her preaching in the woods until her voice strengthened. So into the woods I went, preaching week after week. A change did take place; my voice became fuller and more rounded. I also did some voice training with a few teachers who taught me how to use my diaphragm effectively. As to rehearsing my sermons, I've never done that.

RCJ: What is the next area of your preaching that you will be seeking to develop?

HW: Once, I asked my good friend Dr. Barry Black how I may go about developing myself as a preacher. He gave me the best advice anyone has ever given me in terms of preaching. Dr. Black told me that I should pay attention to the best comedians and how they connect with their audiences. Black pointed out that if comedians fail to connect with their audiences, they may not get paid, and certainly will not be invited back. Yet, because comedians nowadays are so profane, it has been difficult for me to find one I can study and learn from.

RCJ: Which person, experience, book, or commentary has had the greatest influence on your preaching?

HW: Without a doubt, it has been Ella Mitchell's *Those Preaching Women*. William Willimon also had a great impact on me. Willimon mentored me when I received a fellowship from the Episcopal College of Preachers to study preaching, and I was privileged to read a lot of his rich material.

RCJ: As someone who has a doctorate in preaching, where do you see preaching heading in the 21st century?

HW: Everything I say in answering this question must be understood against the backdrop that I am not a foreteller. I believe that preaching will be more prophetic in terms of content, standing in the gap in the tradition of Paul and Peter. After all, it must be as we near the return of our Lord and Savior, Jesus Christ. Preachers will engage in prophetic preaching even if it means they'll be thrown in jail for it. Prophetic preaching is not necessarily shouting the counsel of God, but living what you preach.

RCJ: What counsel do you have for young preachers?

HW: Try not to copy anybody. I happen to like T. D. Jakes personally even though I do not resonate with all of his theology. Jakes assumes a prophetic role when he stands in the pulpit, and he refuses to be like anybody else. Jakes says, "Why would anyone want to be a good copy when he or she can be an incredible original." Even though we need mentors, we must find our own niche. I would also counsel young preachers to get to know God fully so that they can speak out of that center. We must accept that time spent in personal devotions, time passed in getting to know God better, will pay richer dividends than time spent attending preaching conventions intended to only sharpen skills. Finally, I would counsel them to stubbornly resist the temptation to be the top preacher because they probably never will be. Yet if they doubt their natural abilities and rely wholly on God, they will be effective. At least that has been my experience.

The Sermon

"The God of All Types"

A little over a year ago, George Barna did a weekend workshop for us. One of the things I recall Barna telling us about was his survey of churches in America. Barna surveyed a wide array of churches, from small churches of a couple hundred members to mega-churches of several thousand members. Shockingly, Barna discovered that a significant number of church members stated that they did not have a personal relationship with God. What a tragedy! What about you? Do you have a personal relationship with God? Do you know Jesus personally?

Believe it or not, there was a time when Moses, the great deliverer, did not have a personal relationship with God. In Exodus 3 we have the account of Moses encountering the burning bush. When Moses saw the bush burning, he went over to examine it. It was never his intention to find God there. He investigated the burning bush from a scientific standpoint, with a mind that had been trained in the sciences. He was not looking for God. Yet Moses encountered God in that burning bush. As he drew closer to God, Moses was instructed to remove his shoes in reverence, and to encourage him for the assignment he was about to be given, God told Moses: "I am the God of your father, the God of Abraham, the God of Isaac and the God of Jacob" (Gen. 3: 6).

What God taught Moses is important for us today. What God taught Moses at the burning bush is that God is the God of all types. It is important for this generation of believers to understand that, because no two people have the same personality. We do not act the same way. Some folk are like me—sanguine and very dramatic. My God is dramatic, the kind who flashes lightnings. If you are phlegmatic like my friend, your God is peaceful and calm. If your temperament is choleric, then your God is a commanding God. If you're melancholy like Isaac, who I am going to talk about more in a while, your God is a fearful God. So, because of our temperaments, we all have a different view of who God is.

Yet God wants us to know today that He is the God of all personalities and temperaments. God is the God of all types.

In verse 6 of Genesis 3, God begins by telling Moses, " I am THE God . . ." Please underline the emphasis placed on the word *THE*. We live in a generation when God has been relegated to being *A* god. God is just one of many gods. God wanted Moses to know that He is the God who rises above every other God. He is the God whose name cannot be pronounced. He is YHWH. This is powerful stuff, and I am sure that by this time Moses was sitting down. You cannot stand up to this kind of revelation.

God proceeds to inform Moses that He is the God of his father. Do you know that Moses had problems with his father? All of you who have problems with your mothers and fathers, I want you to know that Moses had problems with his dad. When Moses wrote the book of Exodus, he failed to mention the name of his father. I am able to resonate with that. When I wrote my life story, I deliberately left out all mention of my father, prompting many people to question me as to why. The reason I mentioned up to my dog and not my father is because I had unresolved issues with him. My dad abandoned me as a child, and I had not forgiven him when I wrote my autobiography. I thought in leaving him out I would get even with him, and even though he was dead by the time the book was published, I thought his relatives would note that he had not been mentioned.

This is what Moses did. In Exodus 2, Moses writes: "Now a man from the house of Levi went and married a daughter of Levi . . ." This is the way in which Moses refers to his father, the man with whom he lived for the first twelve years of his life, according to Ellen White in *Patriarchs and Prophets*. Undoubtedly, Moses had a problem with his father, so much so that even when Moses was converted, the mention he makes of his father is not all that glowing but cogent and succinct. Talking of his father later, Moses writes: "And Amram married his father's sister Jochebed, and she bore him Aaron and Moses; and the length of Amram's life was one hundred and thirty-seven years" (Gen. 6:20).

The story is told of a famous man who kept journal upon journal detailing every aspect of his life. He had married a woman against the wishes of his family, and the relationship was rocky and tempestuous. The man's diary had only one entry of his wife, and that was the mention of the day she died.

This seems to be what Moses was doing here. Yet God says to Moses that He is the God of his father, too. Amram was not just an ordinary man. He was the strong, silent type. He was the type some of you are; he was the type who does not tell other family members how much they are loved. He was the type who does not embrace others. Maybe Amram never told Moses how he worried about him during the time the Pharoah was plotting the death of the Hebrew males, and maybe Moses grew up believing his father did not love him. And there are some strong, silent types in this congregation who have never told their children that they love them. There are strong, silent Amramites here who've never put their arms around their children.

The sacred record informs us that the priesthood came through Amram. It was because of Amram's commitment to God that the Levis became priests. God chose Aaron, Amram's first son, to be the first high priest. Not only was Amram committed to God, but he chose to live in obscurity. You see, even though he founded the priesthood, he gave the name of his grandfather, Levi, to the priesthood.

So, God wants us to know this morning that He is the God of the strong, silent type. Some of us are from that generation that was told that feelings and emotions are not to be communicated, and today your adult children are people in need of being touched. God is saying to you today that He is your God, and that you must arise and hug your child. It is not enough to hug the pastor at church; you must go home and hug your child, even your adult child. And some of you sitting here today need to be hugged.

But God is not only the God of the silent type, God is also the God of the super hero. God told Moses that He was the God of Abraham (Gen. 3: 6). Abraham was called the father of the faithful and the friend of God. We are not sure what Amram thought of God, but everybody knows about Abraham's view of God. We all know that God was Abraham's shield and reward. When Abraham went out in faith, he did so with his shield, and when Abraham returned, it was with his reward. Abraham had a great faith, and he represents those of us whose faith in God is strong. Abraham was a super hero, and God is the God of the super hero.

Still, Abraham had his trying days. He had his painful experiences. Told by God to sacrifice his son, he wandered about looking for the mountain on which he was to sacrifice Isaac. It must have been a heartrending experience. Have you ever been there, super hero? If you are there today, I want you to know that God knows how it feels. God knows how it feels when you must bear your burdens all alone. God knows how it feels to be in need of a hand when none is forthcoming. God understands how it feels to be viewed as a super hero, yet be misunderstood. And he says, "I am the God of the super hero, too."

God is also the God of the Isaac-type. The name Isaac means "He laughs," but if you study the life of Isaac you will note that he never laughed after he was almost sacrificed on Mt. Moriah. He did not live up to his name; he was melancholy. He was scared of his shadow. Isaac became weak in character and timid in personality. He was so protected by his parents that when he was about 40 and ready to marry it was his parents who found him a wife. Isaac was insignificant, unimpressive and quiet. When Jacob described how his father viewed God, Jacob said that God was the fear of his father, Isaac. God was not the love of Isaac, but the fear of Isaac. God was the one to be afraid of. And Isaac had all reason to be afraid of God. Wouldn't you be afraid of God too if your most vivid recollection of God was God telling your dad to lay you out on an altar? Because I would be afraid of that kind of God, I refuse to belittle Isaac. Isaac must have been scared for life.

If you are afraid of anything today, God wants you to know that He is your God. God knows you; He knows the very depths of your heart. Some of you were offered on the altar of lust by your parents. Some of you were offered on the altar of ambition. Your God is not the warm, embracing God.

There was a time in life when I looked down on people who trembled in the presence of God. I no longer do that. I now understand that some people have gone through experiences that cause them to cower and cringe in the presence of God. To such I say, God is the God of your type. God is the God of the timid. God will look out for you and God will protect you for the rest of your life. He is your God.

But God did not stop there. He said to Moses that He was also the God of Jacob, the one who grasped at the heel and supplanted. Jacob represents the smart and the slick, like me. I think I am smart and slick; I think I can outwit God. And if we're really honest about it, that's where we all are. Jacob represents all of us. He is the man of two natures—the carnal and the divine, the political and the pious, the devout and the dishonest. In the church, but not of it. Look at Jacob and you'll see yourself.

Jacob had to face himself and God at the brook, Jabbok. He wrestled with God thinking he could win because of his craftiness and cunning. Trusting in his own strength, he refused to give way, until his side gave out. Only then did he admit that he was no match for God. He could not fight with God in his own strength. And for the first time in his life he had to tell the truth.

God proceeded to change Jacob from the crafty to the confident. God gave Jacob the name Israel, signifying that Jacob wrestled with God and overcame. Yet Jacob did not overcome God, but his own tendency to mislead and lie and dupe and cheat. No longer would he be victimized by the tendency to trick people.

Today, God wants you to know that there is hope for those addicted to cheating and lying. If you are at Jabbok today, wrestling with a life of duplicity, God wants to offer you release and refuge, refreshment and revival. And the wrestling match in which you are caught up is not with God. You would be killed if you were to wrestle with God. Your wrestling match is with yourself, your carnal nature.

Later in the story of Jacob we hear him refer to God as his Rock. This is not because of what Paul says in 1 Corinthians 10, but because of the fact that when he was at his worse, when he was a liar and a cheat and a manipulator, he laid his head upon a pillar. That night God came to him saying, "Jacob, I will be with you always." Jacob concluded that if God could be with him when he was a supplanter and a conniver, God would be with him forever. God would therefore be Jacob's rock.

God is saying to those of you wrestling with issues or yourself today that He is your God and that He is never going to leave you. I believe if Jacob were alive today he'd repeat the words of that well known gospel hymn, Amazing Grace. Listen to the words of the hymn.

Amazing Grace! How sweet the sound,
That saved a wretch like me!
I once was lost, but now am found,
Was blind, but now I see.

'Twas grace that taught my heart to fear,
And grace my fears relieved;
How precious did that grace appear
The hour I first believed!

The Lord has promised good to me,
His word my hopes secure;
He will my shield and portion be
As long as life endures.

Through many dangers, toils, and snares,
I have already come;
'Tis grace hath brought me safe thus far,
And grace will lead me home.

I want to draw your attention to verse four of the song. That's a special verse. God is saying that you have already come through many dangers and snares. How and why can God say this? Because God has already come through for you. It's done! The snare of ambition that makes you put work and life before God and family. You've already come through that because Jesus took care of everything at the cross. The snare and the addiction of sex, food, the internet, and alcohol, God has already brought you through. It's done. Hallelujah! Hallelujah!

I can testify today that God's amazing grace has worked wonders in my life, and I'd like to invite you to stand if God's amazing grace has been at work in your life, too.

God says He's the God of all types. He is the God of the strong, silent type; He is the God of the super hero; He is the God of the fearful and timid; and, yes, God is the God of the cheats and manipulators and connivers. He saves from the uttermost to the guttermost. All personality types may find rest and refuge in him. His arms are broad and expansive; they are able to hold the whole world. They can embrace you.

If you want Christ to be your God today, won't you come forward as we sing all the verses of this wonderful song.

TEN

Benjamin Reaves

Benjamin Reaves is a vice president for the Adventist Health Systems-Sunbelt, located in Orlando, Florida. Prior to this, he was the president of Oakwood College, and prior to that the chair of the Department of Religion and Theology at Oakwood. Without a doubt, Reaves is a prince of preachers. Reaves taught Homiletics at Oakwood for years, influencing a generation of preachers for years to come. He is known for the emphasis he places on asking the two structural questions: "What is the preacher talking about?" and "What is the preacher saying about what he or she is talking about?" Reaves believes that a good sermon may be summed up in the answers to the two questions about the subject and compliment/predicate of the sermon. Reaves is a polished, suave pulpiteer who knows how to powerfully get his messages across with little fanfare. He is known for his ability to preach a full sermon in no more than twenty-five to thirty minutes.

The Interview

RCJ: When did you know that preaching was something you just had to do?

BR: Preaching assumed a kind of permanence in my mind about my last year in academy. By the time I got to college, it was a full force, something I knew I had to do if I were going to be fulfilled and happy.

RCJ: To whom are you indebted as a preacher?

BR: I am indebted to several preachers, Adventist as well as non-Adventists. Not surprisingly, though, Adventist preachers had a greater impact on me. Among the first Adventist preachers to impact me was Elder Rowe, a former pastor of the Ephesus SDA Church in Harlem, New York, and Elder Jeffries, a contemporary of Rowe who pastored the City Tabernacle Church across town. These two men were giants in the pulpit, and I relished listening to them. Elder C. E. Moseley did a Week of Prayer at Pine Forge Academy while I was a student there, and his preaching was so powerful and pointed that I remember his sermons to this day. As a student at Oakwood, I was influenced most by E. E. Cleveland. Interestingly, Elder Cleveland influenced me not so much in terms of his preaching style, but because of his deep spirituality. He was a real model of a committed spiritual life, and his influence helped me to focus on what is really important in the preaching ministry.

RCJ: What specifically impressed you about the other men?

BR: Rowe was a great pastor who was a specialist on the Holy Spirit. Yet he had style, and he was the figure that would come to mind if you tried to picture in your mind's eye a big city preacher. Moseley conveyed a deeply spiritual and a powerful prophetic image. If there were anybody back then who as they say today showed evidences of having the anointing on him, that person was Moseley. It was something being in the presence of the man, who we all knew had disciplined himself both spiritually and physically by the grace of God. And it was not a matter of whether he did the right things or said the right things, either. Moseley had a power that went far beyond that.

RCJ: What is your personal theology of preaching?

BR: Preaching is communicating biblical truth from God, by God's power, for God's saving purpose. The objective of preaching is to motivate people to accept God's will and plan for their lives. The sermon is the vehicle we use to communicate biblical truth. In my Bible is a quote I placed there several years ago that deftly sums up what preaching is. It says, "I bring my best to the Lord and the battle is the Lord's." Often, I read that quote, especially when, from a human standpoint, I'm all caught up in preparing and polishing a sermon.

RCJ: Sermon preparation has been described as tortuous, tormenting, and tedious work. Do you agree or disagree?

BR: In the main, I do, though I couldn't wax as alliterative in saying so as the person who did. After a sermon that has gone particularly well, people are apt to approach me saying, "Preacher, you must love to preach, you must enjoy preaching." Preaching is what I know I've been called to do, and I do enjoy preaching. But preaching is a demanding discipline that I often wish were easier. I wouldn't say that preaching or sermon preparation is tedious work, though.

RCJ: How do you decide what to preach?

BR: Several factors come into play with the decision, the first being the occasion at which I'll be speaking. Other factors include the composition and needs of the audience, current world events, and my own needs. These are the factors that contribute to my decision now that I am an "itinerant" preacher. When I was in pastoral ministry leading a congregation, my decision was driven primarily by the needs of my congregation, which I discovered, for the most part, as I visited and interacted with my people. I did not have a preaching calendar which laid out from Sabbath to Sabbath what I would be preaching months down the road.

RCJ: What is the first task of the preacher as he or she sits down to begin to put the sermon together?

BR: Undoubtedly, the preacher must first prepare himself or herself. Preacher preparation must come before sermon preparation, and preacher preparation must be an on-going activity, not something done sporadically or only when a preaching assignment is imminent. Unfortunately, all too often preacher preparation suffers in the face of sermon preparation, resulting in spiritually starved and malnourished preachers attempting to serve up spiritual food to God's people.

RCJ: How long does it take you, on average, to prepare a sermon? How much reading do you do, which commentaries do you consult, etc., and how do you know a sermon is ready to be preached?

BR: I spend between eight to twelve hours actually writing out a sermon. Sermon preparation, like preacher preparation, is an on-going activity for me. As such, I do a lot of reading, doing so widely and with an homiletical eye. That means that sermon ideas are sparked in a myriad of ways and from myriad sources. The title of a book, a news commentary, a newspaper item, and a *Reader's Digest* story are examples of the type of sources that spark my sermonic ideas. I contend that preachers must develop the art of reading with a homiletical eye. It goes without saying that they should be always equipped with a means of recording the ideas as they emerge. In the old days, we carried notebooks and pens; in today's highly technological society, palm corders and other cutting-edge electronic devices are the way to go.

RCJ: How do you go about packaging the ideas into sermons?

BR: The "actual" preparation of a sermon begins with the asking of the structural questions that H. Grady Davis introduced several years ago– What is the passage talking about, and what is the passage saying about what it is talking about? At this point in the process, Bible commentaries are off limits. I simply want to read the passage several times over in different versions, each time apply the structural questions. Once I have answered the structural questions, I move on to exegetical commentaries, putting off reading homiletical commentaries for later so that my thinking does not become tarnished. I try not to use homiletical commentaries for information about the passage. Lastly, I develop a homiletical outline and put some flesh on the skeleton.

RCJ: How often do you use the original languages in your sermon preparation?

BR: Knowing the original languages certainly facilitates or helps with the hard work, but given the abundance of computer programs available nowadays, a preacher does not have to be skilled in the use of biblical languages to craft a sermon that inspires, motivates, and transforms. Preachers who don't know Hebrew and Greek may certainly use these tools, and all preachers need to remember that the pulpit is not intended to be a showcase for the preacher's proficiency in biblical languages.

RCJ: What is the secret of powerful preaching?

BR: The secret of powerful preaching is total reliance on God. It is remembering, as I stated earlier, that "the battle is the Lord's," something that is a challenge for preachers who are particular about the way they say things. It is so easy for preachers who have developed, in the words of Davis, the "sensual language of look, smell, and taste," to fall to the temptation to think that their effectiveness is in their words. Yet that is not where the power lies. Our help and power comes from the Lord.

RCJ: What early skills and practices do still use today.?

BR: I still write out my sermons, and I am still basically a manuscript preacher. Manuscript preaching still works for me. My gospel is to fight in your armor if it works for you. The "if" is a big one. Let me emphasize that I am saying that preachers must fight in their armors not if their armor is comfortable, but if it works for them. Early in my ministry I discovered that writing out my sermons facilitated language choice and use. Another early skill I still practice in the pulpit today is time management.

RCJ: I take it that manuscript preaching does not inhibit your delivery in any way?

BR: Some years ago I wrote an article for *Ministry* that addressed concerns about preaching with or without notes. My thesis was that the issue is not so much the use or non-use of notes, but knowing HOW to use the manuscript. Honestly speaking, there are not many preachers who know how to use a manuscript effectively, one of the few who do it well being Charles Adams, the venerable pastor of the Hartford Memorial Baptist Church in Detroit, Michigan. No one can say that Adams is not a master at manuscript preaching. And Adams is not a magician when it come to the use of his notes, either. In other words, Adams does not try to hide his notes, neither is there any sleight of hand with him. His notes are there for everybody to see, and everybody knows that he is reading his sermon. Yet Adams is so skilled at reading his sermons while maintaining contact with his audience that few people listening to him on tape will ever know that he reads his sermons.

RCJ: Do you spend more time preparing any one part of your sermon?

BR: I am tempted to say that I spend more time working on the body, although I would turn right around and say that you have to get them with a good introduction, and that if you don't have a good conclusion you will lose them. What I want my listeners to leave with is the "big idea" in my sermon, not be able to repeat my introduction, a great story I may have told, or an illustration I may have used. I want my listeners to be able to state what my sermon was all about.

RCJ: Are you primarily a topical, textual, expository, or narrative preacher?

BR: I love narrative preaching, a genre that is heavily dependent on the skillful use of language. Narrative preaching calls for the ability to "tell the story" in captivating ways, which requires a lot of practice. Another challenge of narrative preaching is being able to stay in the story. The temptation for preachers using the first person is to step outside the story as they try to get their listeners to buy into and understand the story. Of course, the power of a well-told story is that it makes its own application. A narrative preacher has failed if he or she has to say, "So, my brothers and sisters, you see . . ." The audience should see it without you inviting them to see it or explaining it to them.

RCJ: How is preparing to preach for a divine worship service different from preparing to preach at a funeral of graduation ceremony?

BR: Sermons should always to directed at specific targets. I do not believe in generic sermons.

RCJHow has preaching changed since you first started to preach?

BR: Preachers tend to be more free nowadays, and do better at resisting the urge to mimic or imitate others. The media has had a telling impact on preaching, bringing it into our homes where we can experience it without the solemnity or sanctity of the church building. Among Adventist preachers, there is a tendency to do less doctrinal preaching, something that the "saints" would have frown upon in the old days.

RCJ: What is your definition and understanding of black preaching?

BR: First, black preaching is not some monolithic ideal you do or do not do. To argue that black preaching is a particular style of preaching replete with certain songs and tones is to suggest that Howard Thurman was not a black preacher and that Reverend Franklin is the embodiment of the black preaching tradition. While there are particular styles and themes characteristic of black preaching, the genre is not limited to them, as Henry Mitchell so eloquently points out in his work on the subject. At the heart of black preaching is a perspective that grows out of the experience or world view of those who see God as a liberator and Lord who will make things right. We must get away from the belief that if there is no celebration in the sermon the preacher did not engage in black preaching. It is not my blackness that makes me a black preacher, but the life I have lived and the views I have about God and the world around me.

RCJ: A while ago you mentioned that Adventist preachers do not preach many doctrinal sermons any more. How may black SDA preachers be faithful to the black preaching tradition with its emphasis on liberation, and the SDA message with its emphasis on doctrine, prophecy, and reform?

BR: The choice is not between preaching Adventist doctrines and being authentically black in your preaching, but rather having a real sense of one's self, and a real sense of the meaning of the gospel as it is interpreted through the Adventist tradition. I contend that the element of deliverance that is so characteristic of the black preaching tradition is an integral part of the Adventist message. What we as Adventist preachers need to do is a better job of preaching the liberating aspects of our doctrines.

RCJ: Why are you considered a great preacher? What makes you effective in the pulpit?

BR: I wish I knew the answer to both questions. If anything, what makes me effective are biblical authenticity, clarity of ideas, vividness of language, and, most importantly, reliance and dependence on divine help.

RCJ: What will preaching be like a few years from now?

BR: Preaching will continue to be impacted by technology, and I'm not sure how well that is going to work. Not that I not a believer in or user of technology, but I think the jury is still out on how effective technology is in the pulpit. More and more, preachers are using power point to grab and maintain the attention of their audience, and some of them seem to believe that the wizardry and dazzle of their presentations will drive home the truths they wish their audience to accept. I believe that nothing should ever replace opening the Bible in the sight of people and reading from it. I know that I may be somewhat biased on this point, and may even be indicted for being locked in the past, but I am convinced that technology should ever be a servant of the word. Our culture is still looking for something that works, and nothing works like the Word of God.

RCJ: What do you have to say to young preachers? What are some of the pitfalls they should avoid, and some of the practices and disciplines they should cultivate?

BR: First and foremost, preachers should strive to be themselves. A preacher can be himself or herself and still be an effective communicator of the word. I firmly believe that God can take you as you are and make you all that He wants you to be. In fact, God can and will do infinitely more with the preacher who refuses to adopt the mannerisms, styles, or characteristics of another. Whenever young preachers ask me how they may discover who they are I encourage them to conduct an evangelistic campaign. By the end of the second week of a four or six week campaign, the average preacher will abort his or her E. E. Cleveland or C. D. Brooks or whoever act and fall back on what he or she knows best—himself or herself! There's nothing like an evangelistic campaign to cure preachers of pretending and posturing.

RCJ: What else do you have to share with young preachers?

BR: Once, a young preacher informed me that he wanted to be the best preacher ever. How did I respond to that? I told this young, well-intentioned preacher that he did not want that to happen, the reason being that the minute he became the best preacher there ever was, the minute he reached the top of the mountain, he would stop climbing and growing. Additionally, were he to look over his shoulder or back, more than likely he would see others getting closer to him. Rather than being the best there ever was, each preacher should concentrate on being the best that he or she can be. Of course, we understand that we become the best by the grace of God. Recognizing that all we are and do are by the grace of God prevents self-aggrandizement. Public applause has corrupted many a preacher, and has been the downfall of not a few. Preachers should resist the urge to construct their sermons with a view to gaining the applause of the public, accepting that there are times when they have to preach what is in Scripture and not what is popular. Lastly, I would have preachers know that preaching is hard work and that if they do not intend to spend many hours getting to know Jesus better and in the development of their preaching abilities, they should find other work to do. Working at preaching, yet being totally dependent on God in and out of the pulpit, is what preaching is all about.

The Sermon

"The Providence and Power of God"

Scripture is replete with stories that occupy a cherished place in the mind and memory. Most of these stories are full of drama and loom larger than life. They abound with heroes and are attention-getting and riveting. Shadrach, Meshach, and Abednego in Nebuchadnezzar's fiery furnace. Daniel in the Lion's Den. All of us, young and old, love these stories of adventure, intrigue, and suspense, these tales of protagonists and antagonists, these thrillers of good guys and bad guys. In our Scripture passage for consideration today, all of these elements abound.

About that time King Herod laid violent hands upon some who belonged to the church. He had James, the brother of John, killed with the sword (Acts 12: 1-2, NRSV).

It was bad times in Jerusalem. King Herod was on a roll. Like many present-day political leaders, Herod was riding a wave of political popularity. While many of today's political leaders do so by opposing affirmative action, Herod did so by persecuting Christians, all in the name of political expediency disguised as the common good.

After he saw that it pleased the Jews, he proceeded to arrest Peter also. (This was during the festival of Unleavened Bread.). When he had seized him, he put him in prison and handed him over to four squads of soldiers to guard him, intending to bring him out to the people after the Passover (Acts 12: 3-4, NRSV).

Herod had Peter arrested and took ominous actions that made the ruler's evil intentions all but obvious. Peter was in prison to stay. He would not leave that prison until he was carried out to die. Now, at this point in my study, I was able to feel this sermon coming together on this matter of prison. You see, in very personal ways, we are all very familiar with prisons.

There are all kinds of prisons. Prisons are not just physical, structural things. There are prisons we all know about. They are the obvious ones. Then there are prisons of which only we as individuals know. Additionally, there are prisons of which we do not know fully, and those we refuse to admit even to ourselves.

What's your prison? What's your prison?

Is your prison the solitary confinement of failed or flawed performance? Have you been locked up in driving for the attention and/or approval of others? Have you been seeking affirmation or applause in the clothes you wear, the money you have, and the grades you make. Have you been doing hard time in the never ending struggle to make it? Are you incarcerated in the prison of performance?

Or are you in the Sing Sing of the past? So many here today are prisoners locked in the jail house of the past, the negative past filled with the tragic shadows of yesterday's rejection, ridicule, failure, and abuse.

What's your prison?

Is your prison the San Quentin of the predictions of others? Are you crippled by predictions of your potential for failure in the future? Or is your prison the Alcatraz of peer worship instead of God worship?

What's your prison?

We all have our prisons. What's your prison?

Are you today in the prison of grief? Does your heart lie buried in a grave? Is your prison the solitary confinement of secret sin? Are you a prisoner of your passions? Have you been put away by sex, alcohol, drugs?

Sometime ago I read of a very successful television writer who was earning over $6,500 a week. An experiment with drugs plunged him into a downward spiral of drug abuse. He sunk so low that even as his wife was on the delivery table giving birth to their daughter, he was twenty feet away in a Men's Room injecting a hit of heroin into his body. One month later, he took his infant daughter on a run to buy some heroin in the city's crime-ridden area. On the way home he was stopped by the police for speeding. The arresting officer spotted his baby in the back seat and a hypodermic syringe on the front seat. Staring coldly into the eyes of the addict, the officer exclaimed: "I'm not going to take you in because wherever you are now is worse than anywhere we can put you."

What's your prison?

The fact is that it doesn't matter where we were born, the upbringing we had, the cruel names we were called, what people may have done to us, the trouble into which we got, how low we sank, or how far behind we may have fallen. The fact is that God opens prisons doors.

So this passage is about more than prison. This passage is about God's power. Can't you feel it coming together?

Hallelujah. Hallelujah. Here's where we can celebrate, for whatever the prison, God is able to deliver. God is the God who opens prison doors.

In the case of Peter, Herod took no chances. Herod deployed four relays of at least four soldiers to surround Peter. There was a soldier on each side of the apostle, and two more at the door of his cell. And these soldiers were there around the clock. Clearly, there was no way of escape for the apostle.

The very night before Herod was going to bring him out, Peter, bound with two chains, was sleeping between two soldiers, while guards in front of the door were keeping watch over the prison. Suddenly an angel of the Lord appeared and a light shone in the cell. He tapped Peter on the side and woke him, saying, "Get up quickly." And the chains fell off his wrists. The angel said to him, "Fasten your belt and put on your sandals." He did so. Then he said to him, "Wrap your cloak around you

and follow me." Peter went out and followed him; he did not realize that what was happening with the angel's help was real; he thought he was seeing a vision. After they had passed the first and second guard, they came before the iron gate leading into the city. It opened for them of its own accord, and they went outside and walked along a lane, when suddenly the angel left him. Then Peter came to himself and said, "Now I am sure that the Lord has sent his angel and rescued me from the hands of Herod and from all that the Jewish people were expecting" (Acts 12: 6-11, NRSV).

The powerful truth is that the God of the Bible is a God who is able to open prison doors. So this story is not just about prison, or being in prison. No, no, no. This story is more about power; it is about God's marvelous, matchless, magnificent, and awesome power.

We tend to zip through this narrative and rush to this dramatic, astounding, incredible, and miraculous part. But before we rush from the pain of prison to rejoice in the comfort of God's power, we need to struggle with the challenge of God's providence. And, believe me, there is a challenge here. While it may appear that the chapter has ended, there remains a challenge. There is a question, a troubling concern that remains, yea, that cries out for attention. You see, while Peter was delivered, James, the brother of John, was killed with the sword.

Like Peter, James had been prayed for. The church prayed for James, too. Yet, unlike Peter, James was not delivered. He was put to death by sword, which is just a diplomatic and courteous way of saying that James was beheaded.

Help me, somebody!!! How do I get a handle on this? I desperately need to understand this. Was Peter more deserving of life than James? What did James do that deserved the death penalty be carried out? Why did James fall through the cracks? Was God's miraculous power only reserved for Peter? Weren't these two men just as deserving of God's pardon and mercy?

Let's bring it a little closer home. Let's make it a little more current, a little more contemporary. One young man is miraculously delivered from a horrendous auto accident while another is not. Why? What is the reason for this? A loved one dies from cancer; yet someone else is healed. Why?

Please help me, somebody. How do I go about getting a handle on this? Where is the sense in this? Can it be that when we pray for deliverance from problems, heartaches, and healing that our limited view of time and eternity narrows our perceptions of what an answer should be? Did God hear the prayers for Peter and not the ones for James?

Sometimes, discouragement over what we perceive as unanswered prayer in the past wilts our willingness to pray boldly. We assume that there was no answer because what happened was not what we wanted. We get caught up in judging God on the basis of what we thought God should do or what God should have done.

Well, this passage is clear; it is quite obvious. Peter was delivered, and James was executed. What this demonstrates is that divine providence is not some cookie cutter that can be manipulated by our prayers.

I am wary of those television gospel con men who claim to have divine providence down pat. They claim to have catalogued and correlated the doings and dealings of God, and they offer up cute, glib, little, sound byte answers to your heartache. These individuals have not been perceptive enough to realize that God does not move on our timetables. They have not discerned that some of God's operations do not add up on man-made calculators.

Maybe the little boy who didn't understand why God put so many vitamins in spinach and did not put more of them in ice cream had a revelation after all. That revelation is that things do not always fit together in just the way we think they should. Doors are not always opened on our time schedule. Jesus Himself prayed, "Let this cup pass from me," and it didn't. Our God opens those doors that He determines needs opening. And this is a matter of trusting God's providence and sovereignty. True faith is not blind to the realities of the situation, nor to the fact that God works out His purposes in the ways that God chooses. True faith recognizes and accepts that God retains the right to act as God sees fit.

True faith is not in deliverance. True faith is in our God. Like the Hebrew boys testified, our God is able to deliver, but if God chooses not to, we are still confident of God's power. And we keep on trusting God's providence even if deliverance does not come.

That kind of faith means trusting God and God's word. It means believing without seeing, and knowing without feeling. It does not mean that we know or understand what God's specific purpose in our lives may be. It is a trusting willingness to follow God whatever God's purpose, whatever the path of God's providence.

Now, let's go back to that prison with its massive rock-hewn cell, that prison with its bars, bolts, and Roman guards. See it clearly, in your mind's eye. Peter knew that God was able to deliver. He knew that the church was praying for him as they had for James. And he knew what had happened to James. Yet the apostle trusted God's providence. How do I know it? Because he laid down and went to sleep.

One of my favorite photos is a picture of me holding my first grandchild, Marcia, a few months after she was born. The picture is of a tiny, helpless grandchild resting peacefully in the arms of her loving grandfather.

What a picture of trust and serenity we have in that prison cell. Sleep for Peter was so sound and so sweet that the angel had difficulty waking him up. The peace that passes all understanding comes only on trust in God's power and trust in God's providence.

I must confess that if it had been me in that prison cell, the soldiers would not have gotten a wink of sleep because of my tossing and turning all night long. My rattling chains would have kept them up. While it is true that sometimes children have nightmares, it is unarguably true that grown-up children experience the same. We need to be reminded that God works the night shift.

If God delivers us, we must praise God and continue to trust. Yet, if God does not deliver us, we should praise God and continue to trust God still.

It seems to me that when it's the prison of spiritual enslavement, God's providence exercises God's power without delay, but that other than that we have to face the reality of divine timing, delay, or decision. Still, we must do so like Peter, snoring away, serenely submissive to God's will, and trusting in God's power and providence.

I like the way a gospel recording artist put it. "I've got confidence God's going to see me through. No matter what the way may be, I know He's going to fix it for me " (Andrae Crouch).

When we settle the trusting of God's providence, then we are prepared to celebrate God's power as manifested in the ways God's providence determines what is best for our lives and for the larger drama of God's eternal plan.

This episode then is not a story of God's providence or God's power. It is a story of God's providence **AND** God's power. Both are exhibited in the lives of James who died and Peter who was delivered.

It was an electric moment. A Sabbath service at the Breath of Life Church in Washington, D. C. was in progress. The Voices of Zion and their soloist were singing "He keeps right on blessing me." The selection was profoundly moving. Yet the impact of the song was heightened beyond measure when I realized that the soloist singing with every ounce of his soul was blind.

Do you think there was a time when James could not say "He keeps right on blessing me?" What about you? Trusting God means that there is no experience in which we cannot say "He keeps right on blessing me."

ELEVEN

G. Ralph Thompson

G. Ralph Thompson was born in Barbados and became a Seventh-day Adventist while studying at Caribbean Union College in Trinidad, W.I. He went on to become a successful pastor, college teacher, college president, union president and a vice president of the General Conference of Seventh-day Adventists. He was secretary of the General Conference until 2000, when he began to work for the Ellen G. White Estate at the denomination's world headquarters. As a pastor/evangelist in the Caribbean, Thompson was known for his pointed, poignant, penetrating preaching. Indeed, it was his preaching that catapulted him into international prominence. As a leader working at the General Conference, Thompson has preached around the world, never failing to hold his hearers in rapt attention. Thompson's sermon, "Knowing the Time," was delivered at the General Conference Session in 2000. First printed in the *Adventist Review*, it is reprinted here with the permission of the author.

The Interview

RCJ: You've been preaching for over fifty years. How did you get started?

GRT: I was not a Seventh-day Adventist when I enrolled at Caribbean Union College in Trinidad in the mid-1940s, but shortly after I arrived on campus, in 1946 to be exact, I was baptized. Once I became a Seventh-day Adventist, I began associating with and listening to preachers, and it was not long that a growing feeling and conviction that I should be a preacher came over me.

RCJ: Which preacher did you admire and wish to be like back then?

GRT: Because radio was always an interest of mine, H. M. S. Richards, Sr.

of the Voice of Prophecy Radio Broadcast was one of my favorite preachers. I also fell in love with Harold Nembhard after he conducted a Week of Prayer at the College in 1948. Nembhard, an outstanding evangelist in the Caribbean at the time, was brought in by the College administration to conduct the Week of Prayer in the wake of some student unrest, and I remember him appealing to the students and administrators to come together in love and understanding. I had the good fortune to be his intern when I graduated in 1950. It was both a pleasure and an inspiration to work with him.

RCJ: What was your first preaching experience like?

GRT. There was a ministerial club at the college that met every Friday evening to hear and critique the sermon of a student. We took turns preaching. My baptism into the ministerial fire of preaching occurred on one such occasion. I was young and inexperienced, but so were those critiquing me. I remember my peers being very kind to me, even going so far as saying that they had been blessed. I was impressed with the fact that preaching could be a very meaningful experience, and I became convinced that I could spend the rest of my life doing it. In time, I developed my preaching skills and became very comfortable at the task.

RCJ: How do you define preaching, and what is your theology of preaching?

GRT: Preaching is taking a message from God's Word, letting it penetrate your heart and soul, and then delivering it to God's people. The message has to grip the preacher before it can impact the people of God. So, by way of a formal definition, a sermon is God's message, preached by God's men or women, to God's people.

RCJ: What's your method of sermon preparation? Please share your step-by-step approach?

GRT: The way I prepare sermons has changed over the years. I suppose that is to be expected. When I started preaching, I use to write out my sermons word for word, doing so because I wanted the language to be just right. I was impressed with the fact that if I was able to write out what I wanted to say, especially a vital point, it wouldn't slip my mind in the pulpit. For evangelistic sermons, however, I used outlines. Either way, I would study my passage extensively, going over the text in several translations before going to the commentaries. I still follow this practice today. With my material laid out before me, I formulate a thesis, construct an outline, and put the flesh on the skeleton. Let me add that several years in administration drastically cut down on the time I had to do in-depth research.

RCJ: Where do you look for illustrations?

GRT: I love to read biographies and autobiographies, finding in them treasures of information that can be used as illustrations. Of course, after half a century of traveling and preaching, I get much of my illustration material from my own experiences.

RCJ: You mentioned that in the early days of your ministry you wrote out your sermons word for word. What kind of preacher are you today—manuscript, outline, or extemporaneous? And what difference do you think these various modes of delivery make?

GRT:Even though I write out my sermons, I try not to use many notes in the pulpit, knowing that maintaining eye contact makes for maximum impact of the sermon. I particularly enjoy doing an exposition of a passage with little more than the Bible with me.

RCJ: Do you ever rehearse your sermons, preaching them out loud before delivering them?

GRT:Your question brings back to memory a practice I had while I was a Seminary student in Washington, D. C. Often while I drove back and forth between D. C. and New York City, where many of my close friends lived, I'd preached to myself. Of course, I would do this when I was alone. In the four hours it took me to go from one city to another, I'd preach several sermons, complete with appeals and all. On many occasions passing motorists looked at me quizzically, as though I was crazy. I do not follow this practice today, preferring to preach my sermons in my head.

RCJ: How much time do you spend in silent mediation and practicing the spiritual disciplines?

GRT:As one who was a church administrator for several years, I know how vital it is to guard well the time that should be spent pursuing God through prayer and meditation. By nature I am a person who listens more than one who talks, even doing more listening than talking on committees. I wish I could be more talkative, something with which my wife agrees. So listening to the Lord comes naturally for me. I've discovered that if you are going to do a lot of talking for the Lord, you must do a lot of listening to the Lord. I've learned how to maximize the hours in the day listening to the Lord, using the "dead time" often spent waiting in airports and traveling to communicate with the Lord. God can speak to us in all kinds of places and under all sorts of conditions.

RCJ: How do you make the distant past of Scripture relevant to your listeners?

GRT:Much of what took place in the distant past of Scripture is repeated in some form today. As the wise man so aptly puts it, "There is nothing new under the sun." Given that reality, making the distant past of Scripture relevant today is not as monumental an undertaking as some people think it is. Still, the challenge for the preacher is to scratch where the people are itching. We must make sure that when our listeners leave the sanctuary they go away with the wherewithal to face the challenges of the week facing them.

RCJ: Do you spend more time working on any one part of the sermon?

GRT: The sermon is an integrated whole, but if I had to, I would spend more time on the body of the sermon. To be sure, the introduction gets you started and leads you right into the body of the sermon, but the body deals with your major points, your thesis, if you please. It is in the body that you drive home what you what your listeners to go away with. The body addresses the challenges and implications of your message. In the conclusion you aim to make your hearers make a decision. You are seeking to have them implement what they have heard, to make it applicable to their personal experience. Yet if you have failed to prove your point in the body of the sermon, your conclusion and appeal will fall flat. I would say, therefore, that the body is the most important part of the sermon and requires the most intense work.

RCJ: How do you rebound from a "bad sermon day?"

GRT: There is no such thing as a "bad sermon day." Now, it is true that I have preached sermons that left me feeling I was not on target, that something was missing. Yet often when we think that we didn't "hit it" somebody comes up to us afterward and says, "The Lord really blessed me today. Something you said inspired me." I have had people tell me of sermons I preached years ago, often quoting verbatim what I said, when I felt as though I missed the mark. If there is anything good to be said about feeling somewhat low after a sermon, it is that the feeling motivates you to be better prepared the next time.

RCJ: How do you prevent your confidence from degenerating into arrogance or cockiness?

GRT: The preacher must ever remember that whatever he or she is able to effect in the pulpit is all due to the power of God. Also, somewhere out there there is a preacher who is better at the craft. If nothing else, these two facts should keep a preacher humble. Throughout my ministry my personal philosophy has been, "Keep your feet on the ground." Consequently, all through my service to the church as a college professor, college president, union president, and General Conference secretary, I made sure never to forget that God was the reason for my success.

RCJ: What is your understanding of black preaching?

GRT: Coming from the Caribbean, the idea of black preaching threw me at first. In Barbados, where I was born, and in Trinidad, where I lived for seventeen years, ours was a conservative religion that was heavily influenced by English traditions that we prized. Some of us were confused by the idea of totally black and white churches in this country because we did not have that experience when we left the Caribbean, where we, black folk, were in the majority. I soon resonated with my black brothers and sisters in this country, where the reverse is true. In other words, whites, who are in the majority, have the money, power, and control here, and the black minority, especially in the days of Jim Crowism and apartheid, is discriminated against. I've said all of that to say that black preaching is preaching that comes out of the black experience.

RCJ: What distinguishes black preaching from other types of preaching?

GRT: Black preaching is preaching that makes the text come alive. It is a powerful tool and resource that utilizes words to paint pictures that the eyes can almost visibly see. Black preaching is preaching that hits the nail on the head. Our brothers in North America are adroit at it, and among Seventh-day Adventist colleges and universities in North America, none can compete with Oakwood College in terms of graduating giant black preachers.

RCJ: In 2000, Dr. Calvin B. Rock wrote an article about black preaching for *Ministry* Magazine in which he argues that black preaching is more content than style. Do you agree?

GRT: I totally agree. Henry Mitchell, who has written extensively on the subject, bemoans the fact that some black preachers put more emphasis on style. He argues that style should grow out of content, and that it is the content of the sermon that forms the basis for celebration. The fact of the matter is that methodology can sometimes cause people to miss the content of your sermon, and it is sad when that happens.

RCJ: Are we black Seventh-day Adventist or Seventh-day Adventist preachers who are black?

GRT: We are, first of all, Seventh-day Adventist preachers. I was ordained to be a Seventh-day Adventist preacher, something I remind preachers of whenever I am privileged to speak at an ordination service. I was not ordained to be a Baptist, Methodist, or Church of God preacher, but to be an Adventist who preaches the everlasting gospel in the context of the three angels' messages. My preaching, therefore, must make the pulpit supremely and uniquely Seventh-day Adventist. My sermons must not be those that can be preached any and everywhere, but those that have what we call the "Great Controversy" themes running through them. And, as I often say, the Seventh-day Adventist message that I accepted when I was 17 years old it still relevant today.

RCJ: How has preaching changed in the half a century you've been preaching, and what will it be like in the 21st century?

GRT: Fifty years ago most preachers were topical, using the proof-text method to drive home the truths they were trying to prove. That kind of preaching tended to make a legalist of the preacher, and, thank God, changed over the years. Expository preaching and narrative preaching reigned supreme in the second half of the 20th century. I am happy to see preachers staying in the Word today, aspiring to be thoroughly biblical. Preaching that places an emphasis on teaching is very much in vogue today, with the preacher often using a glass pulpit from which he or she is prone to walk away to maintain contact with the congregation and to stress his or her authenticity.

RCJ: What is the challenge for Seventh-day Adventist preachers?

GRT: The mandate from Ellen White is that as Adventist preachers we must lift up Christ in every sermon. Our tendency to make a dichotomy between doctrine and Christ is false, because the greatest doctrine in Scripture is Jesus Christ. The doctrine of the State of the Dead is nothing apart from the fact that there is life in Jesus Christ, the foundation of immortality. And the Sabbath is nothing if it is not that Jesus Christ is the Lord of the Sabbath. Our challenge is to make Jesus Christ the foundation and content of every sermon and doctrine we preach.

RCJ: Why are you ranked among Adventism's great preachers? What makes for your effectiveness?

GRT: I don't know that I have an answer to these two questions. Yet, if people consider me a great Adventist preacher, it may be because of the positions I held at the General Conference. When you are at the GC, people expect you to be a good speaker. It doesn't matter how good a committee member you are. You are expected to deliver in the pulpit.

RCJ: How would you like to be remembered as a preacher?

GRT: As a Christ-centered preacher. "There is no name under heaven given among men whereby we must be saved." Christology is still my thing; I believe in preaching and uplifting Christ. That is all we should do in every sermon.

RCJ: What advice do you have for budding preachers? What are some to the pitfalls they should avoid, and the practices and disciplines they should cultivate, if they are going to succeed being Christ-centered, Spirit-filled preachers?

GRT: To put it in North American terms, they should watch out for two major threats—honey and money. Many of our great preachers have been destroyed because of unacceptable relationships with individuals of the opposite sex. I remind preachers that some of the people after them wouldn't look at them if they were not preachers. The second thing that has destroyed many of our pastors is money.

RCJ: Is there anything else you'd like to share?

GRT:Preachers must to be content with what the Lord has done for them, stubbornly resisting the temptation to compare themselves to others. God knows why you've been entrusted with the gifts you have. Additionally, budding preachers must pray for strength to conquer discouragement, an emotion that has bedeviled the greatest of preachers and to which preachers are especially vulnerable when they feel they've not done as well as they had hoped to in the pulpit. Lastly, I'd counsel budding preachers to stay on their knees, and in a deep and abiding relationship with God and God's people.

The Sermon

"Knowing the Time"

In Romans 13, Paul outlines the duties of the Christian believer in society: "Let every soul be subject to the government authorities. . . . Render therefore to all their due: taxes to whom taxes are due, customs to customs, fear to whom fear, honor to whom honor" (Rom. 13:1-7 NKJV).

Why is the Christian to do all these things? Why is the Christian to be a good citizen? The answer is outlined in verses 11-14: "And do this, knowing the time, that now is high time to awake out of sleep; for now our salvation is nearer than when we first believed."

What time is it? When we look around us, we see a world in revolt, enveloped in violence, destruction, and protest. The old norms of conduct are no longer respected, the old cliches no longer work, the old formulas no longer produce the results they used to.

In this technological, computerized age, the world has become one global village. Knowledge has increased with incredible speed. All the scientific wonders of the past have now coalesced, forming a peak upon which to stand ready to hurl this generation into the full and final glory of human scientific outreach. Once it was the moon we aimed for, then it was the planets, next time it will be the stars. After that, who knows?

What Time Is It?

It's the time when humans will keep on pressing their claim for the conquest of outer space. This age of scientific exploration is indeed the great second renaissance, the glory of which is destined to reach its peak in our generation.

It's the time of a new religion abroad in the land, a religion created by science. The computer, satellite communication, and the communication highway are causing millions of their devotees to bow the knee in adoration. This new religion makes us into our own god, worshiping at the shrine that we have dedicated to ourselves. As one scientist has said, science has opened the gateway to heaven.

In the area of morality we have reached a new low. Collapsing moral standards are strewn in great profusion along the pathway of our decadent society. The moorings have been removed, and we are being buffeted back and forth by the winds of loose passion, sexual promiscuity, marital infidelity, and the so-called new morality. This ever-rising flood of immorality threatens to engulf all of society. The few minority voices raised in alarm at the approaching disaster sound strangely off-key and unreal. In fact, very few are even listening or concerned. We cannot begin to fathom the great depths of moral decay into which our society has fallen. We even have the sad spectacle of clergy and religious leaders putting their approval on homosexuality and premarital sexual relations. Such is the situation that even the clergy is brainwashed and sin is being called righteousness. Our cities are sick, our society is sick, our generation is sick. A terrible plague has broken out in epidemic proportions, and a moral cesspool threatens to engulf us all.

And what is the picture like in the field of religion? I wish things were brighter here. I wish I could tell you that there is evidence of a great revival. Unfortunately, the opposite is true. Religion in general has become formal, dead, and arctic-like. Here and there can be found a little stirring and flurry. But the cruel fact is that the church in general is not being taken seriously by the world at large. To most people, God is dead. Most religious people are content to have their ministers drug them to sleep on Sunday mornings, and sometimes Sabbath mornings, with some soporific potion of attractive, secularistic, materialistic, and ecumenistic concoction. Religion, for most people, is something to be put on and taken off like a coat, to be worn only in church. It must not affect their private lives. They want just enough religion to cover them with a veneer of respectability.

It is time for us as Seventh-day Adventists to go out into this sick and dying world and declare the binding claims of God's holy law as exemplified in the life of Christ. "The night is far spent, the day is at hand. Therefore let us cast off the works of darkness, and let us put on the armor of light. Let us walk properly, as in the day, not in revelry and drunkenness, not in lewdness and lust, not in strife and envy. But put on the Lord Jesus Christ, and make no provision for the flesh, to fulfill its lusts" (verses 12-14). God's remedy for sin is found in Jesus Christ. In this battered, bleeding, sin-sickened, dying world of ours, we confidently point men and women to the soon return of Jesus Christ our Lord.

So Little Time

Time is running out on us. It could very well be that we are nearer to the coming of Christ than we even think! Ours is a wonderful opportunity to witness with our own eyes the fulfillment of Bible prophecy. This is the period that is destined to witness the climax of the ages.

Today the human race finds itself sitting on top of a rumbling volcano and crying out desperately, "What shall we do?" Brothers and sisters, this is our opportunity to tell them that all things are now ready for the return of heaven's King and that the kingdoms of this world are soon to become the kingdom of our Lord and of His Christ. As James Stewart of Edinburgh, Scotland, once said: "Our task is to confront the rampant disillusionment of today and smash it with the cross of Christ and shame it with the splendor of the resurrection." And, I add, shatter it with the glorious news of the second coming of Christ in apocalyptic glory. Whatever department of the church we serve, this is the touchstone of our hopes, the raison d'etre of our service, the ultimate consummation of our earnest desires.

Now let me say this, my fellow Seventh-day Adventist Church employees: we must not be mercenary servants; we do not work just for the dollars and cents. Our service for God and His church is based on His love for us and our love for Him.

Permit me also to say a word to our vast number of highly educated, beautiful young people of this church. You have great talent that God can use in the proclamation of His message and the finishing of His work on earth. You should bring to the cause of God an alert mind, a dedicated life, and a surplus of good common sense. What a great blessing it is to the church for our young people to be well trained academically, and then have that training baptized by the Holy Spirit! I say to you today, young people, get all the education you can and then use it for the glory of God.

In the *Advent Review and Sabbath Herald* of November 13, 1913, Ellen G. White wrote: "All heaven is astir, engaged in preparing for the day of God's vengeance, the day of Zion's deliverance. The time of tarrying is almost ended. The pilgrims and strangers who have so long been seeking a better country are almost home. I feel as if I must cry aloud, Homeward bound! Rapidly we are nearing the time when Christ will come to gather His redeemed to Himself."

Brothers and sisters, the times demand that we take an agonizing reappraisal of our objectives and our methods. We must keep pace with the demands of this tremendous hour. This is no time for timid leadership or play-it-safe techniques. The times demand bold, adventuresome, untried methods in order to keep abreast of the exigencies of today.

We are nearing home, and I believe that the revival we so much need will indeed come. There will be a revival among us not seen since the days of Pentecost. It will come with ten times the power of Pentecost. Under the Holy Spirit's outpouring and unction, this Advent movement will not peter out on the rocks of oblivion, but rather it shall gather momentum with every passing day until it reaches a grand and glorious climax.

Send Out the Music

Many years ago John Evelyn visited Amsterdam and went into the Tower of Saint Nicholas to observe the playing of those marvelous chimes. He found a man way below the bells with a type of wooden gloves on his hands pounding away on the keyboards. The nearness of the bells, the clanging of the keys when struck by the wooden gloves, and the clatter of the wires made it impossible for him to hear the music. But many people in the town paused in their work and listened to the chiming and were glad.

And so it may be, fellow laborer, that in your watchtowers when you are wearily pouring the music of your lives out into the empty lives of others, the rattling of the keys, the heavy hammers, the twanging of the wires, and the very nearness of the work may all conspire to prevent you from catching the music. But across the crowded cities and villages full of weary sin-sick souls, and far out on the eternal sea, the melody of your work will blend with the song of the angels. Do not ever be discouraged in your work for the Master.

Those who have stood on the heights above the city of Naples, Italy, tell us that as the sound comes up from that populous city and reaches the upper air, it meets and mingles on a minor key. There are the voices of traffic and of command; the voices of affection and rebuke, the shouts of sailors and cries of itinerant vendors in the street, as well as the chatter and laughter of children. But they all come up, forming an indistinguishable moan in the air.

That moan in the air is the voice of the world as it reaches the throne of God. It is a cry for help. Christ, who poured out His soul unto death that the world might be saved, hears that cry and waits with unutterable longing for souls to hear the message, for channels through which His divine love can flow to every part of the world. Will you become involved in its proclamation? Will you go forward with fortitude and resolute purpose to point men and women heavenward? I believe God is counting on you and me, for He has made no other plans.

Time to Act

Now is the time and, thank God, we are the people. I am sure that we all recognize that we have come to the now time. If ever the time was auspicious for striking out for God, it is now! If ever the time was ripe for the harvest, it is now!

Now, while the hearts of humanity are failing them for fear; now, when men and women have become disillusioned with the fleeting pleasures of earth; now, when the universal cry is for something lasting and eternal; now, while the forces of good and evil are consolidating for the last great struggle to the death; now, while science is exploding in ever-breathtaking marvels; now, while men are reaching for the planets of outer space and on to the stars; now, while the doors of opportunity are still open for the preaching of the gospel; now, while the stupefying, crippling, corroding epidemic of sin seems about to envelop the whole of society; now, while the youth of the world are looking for the challenge, something to live for, something to die for; now, while the confused, bewildered masses of earth are groping blindly in the darkness of misery and despair; now, while our decadent society seems bent on destruction; now, while moral laxity and marital infidelity and the new morality are doing their destructive work; now, while the angels of God are holding back the winds of strife from increasing into a global hurricane; now, when the prophecy of Joel concerning the outpouring of God's Spirit upon His people in latter rain proportions is about to be fulfilled; now, in this hour of history, God's call to service comes to each of us to do our part to bring to a great triumphal conclusion the sharing of the Advent message throughout this great, challenging, desperate period of the world's history.

We are a people of prophecy, a people of destiny, a people with a mission, a people with a deadline. We are the people with the message for these times. We are the people of the remnant, and our redemption draweth nigh. The time is ripe, the message is right, and God is ready! The question is, are we ready?

Someone has said the church's whispers must become shouts, her lethargy must become enthusiasm, and her subdued light must become a beacon upon the hilltops of the world. We are the people of the book—we love the Bible. We are the people with a Savior—we love the Lord. We are the people of hope—we look for Christ's return. We are the people of prayer—we talk with God. We are the people of law and order—we love God's commandments. We are the people with the Sabbath—we keep holy the seventh day of the week. We are the people of principle—we hold high standards. We are the people with a program—the globe is our limit. We are the people with a heart—we help the needy. We are the people with a past—we go back to Pentecost. We are the people with a future—heaven is our home.

So, knowing the time, let us awake and join hands together in the glorious proclamation of the third angel's message as it sweeps to its mighty climax.